AMERICAN
WAR LIBRARY

★ ★ ★ ★

★ The Civil War ★

LINCOLN
AND THE ABOLITION
OF SLAVERY

by Russell Roberts

Lucent Books, P.O. Box 289011, San Diego, CA 92198-9011

Titles in The American War Library series include:

World War II
Hitler and the Nazis
Kamikazes
Leaders and Generals
Life as a POW
Life of an American Soldier in
  Europe
Strategic Battles in Europe
Strategic Battles in the Pacific
The War at Home
Weapons of War

The Civil War
Leaders of the North and South
Life Among the Soldiers and
  Cavalry
Lincoln and the Abolition of
  Slavery
Strategic Battles
Weapons of War

Library of Congress Cataloging-in-Publication Data

Roberts, Russell, 1963–
      Lincoln and the abolition of slavery / by Russell Roberts
            p.   cm.—(American war library series)
      Includes bibliographical references and index.
      Summary: Discusses Abraham Lincoln's role in the aboliton of
slavery, including the Civil War and the Emancipation Proclamation.
      ISBN 1-56006-580-X (lib. : alk. paper)
      1. Lincoln, Abraham, 1809–1865—Views on slavery
Juvenile literature. 2. Antislavery movements—United States—
History—19th century Juvenile literature. 3. Slaves—Emancipation
United States Juvenile literature. 4. United States—Politics and
government—1861–1865 Juvenile literature. [1. Emancipation
Proclamation. 2. Antislavery movements. 3. United States—
History—Civil War, 1861–1865. 4. Slavery—History. 5. Lincoln,
Abraham, 1809–1865.] I. Title. II. Series.
973.7'092—dc21   99-23477
                                                                 CIP

✫ Contents ✫

A Nation Forged by War

The United States, like many nations, was forged and defined by war. Despite Benjamin Franklin's opinion that "There never was a good war or a bad peace," the United States owes its very existence to the War of Independence, one to which Franklin wholeheartedly subscribed. The country forged by war in 1776 was tempered and made stronger by the Civil War in the 1860s.

The Texas Revolution, the Mexican-American War, and the Spanish-American War expanded the country's borders and gave it overseas possessions. These wars made the United States a world power, but this status came with a price, as the nation became a key but reluctant player in both World War I and World War II.

Each successive war further defined the country's role on the world stage. Following World War II, U.S. foreign policy redefined itself to focus on the role of defender, not only of the freedom of its own citizens, but also of the freedom of people everywhere. During the cold war that followed World War II until the collapse of the Soviet Union, defending the world meant fighting communism. This goal, manifested in the Korean and Vietnam conflicts, proved elusive, and soured the American public on its achievability. As the United States emerged as the world's sole superpower, American foreign policy has been guided less by national interest and more on protecting international human rights. But as involvement in Somalia and Kosovo prove, this goal has been equally elusive.

As a result, the country's view of itself changed. Bolstered by victories in World Wars I and II, Americans first relished the role of protector. But, as war followed war in a seemingly endless procession, Americans began to doubt their leaders, their motives, and themselves. The Vietnam War especially caused people to question the validity of sending its young people to die in places where they were not particularly wanted and for people who did not seem especially grateful.

While the most obvious changes brought about by America's wars have been geopolitical in nature, many other aspects of society have been touched. War often does not bring about change directly, but acts instead like the catalyst in a chemical reaction, accelerating changes already in progress.

Some of these changes have been societal. The role of women in the United States had been slowly changing, but World War II put thousands into the workforce and into uniform. They might have gone back to being housewives after the war, but equality, once experienced, would not be forgotten.

Likewise, wars have accelerated technological change. The necessity for faster airplanes and a more destructive bomb led to the development of jet planes and nuclear energy. Artificial fibers developed for parachutes in the 1940s were used in the clothing of the 1950s.

Lucent Books' American War Library covers key wars in the development of the nation. Each war is covered in several volumes, to allow for more detail, context, and to provide volumes on often neglected subjects, such as the kamikazes of World War II, or weapons used in the Civil War. As with all Lucent Books, notes, annotated bibliographies, and appendixes such as glossaries give students a launching point for further research. In addition, sidebars and archival photographs enhance the text. Together, each volume in The American War Library will aid students in understanding how America's wars have shaped and changed its politics, economics, and society.

Too Raw a Wound

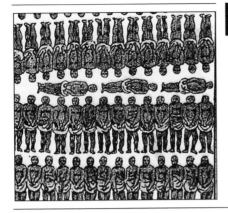

According to historical accounts, the first Africans were brought to America as slaves in August 1619. A Dutch man-of-war ship, captained by a man named Jope, docked at the Jamestown colony in Virginia. In dire need of food, Jope traded his "cargo"—twenty African slaves—for supplies from the colonists and sailed off.

Slavery had begun in America. By the time it ended, nearly 250 years later, it had almost destroyed the United States.

From the moment of its birth, the United States was plagued by strife and controversy over slavery. When Thomas Jefferson wrote the Declaration of Independence, he included a paragraph about slavery, part of which read:

He [the British king] has waged cruel war against human nature itself, violating its most sacred rights of life and liberty in the person of a distant people who never offended him, captivating and carrying them into slavery in another hemisphere, or to incur miserable death in their transportation thither.[1]

These words, which John Adams called a "vehement philippic [tirade] against Negro slavery,"[2] caused an uproar among delegates to the Continental Congress. Representatives from Southern states refused to vote for the declaration if slavery was included as one of the grievances against the king. The offending paragraph was removed.

After the Revolutionary War (during which five thousand blacks served with the Continental army and distinguished themselves in numerous battles, including Bunker Hill and Yorktown), a movement began to abolish slavery in Northern states.

However, because of the economic importance of cotton in the South, slavery remained a viable institution in the Southern states, forcing politicians to continually

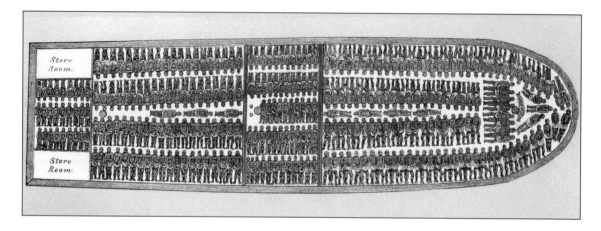

Store Room.

Store Room.

craft compromises to satisfy both anti- and pro-slavery forces. Ultimately, however, all of these compromises failed. Slavery was too volatile an issue, too raw a wound on the body politic of the United States to be successfully papered over by political compromise. As the United States expanded, the problem of slavery cropped up again and again; the slave states wanted to let slavery take root in new territories, while the nonslave states fought to keep these areas free.

By 1850, slavery was a powder keg needing only a spark to ignite it and blow the country apart. A series of crises over slavery during that decade moved the United States to the brink of civil war. John Brown's attempt to incite a slave insurrection by raiding Harpers Ferry, Vir-

This diagram shows the way in which blacks were packed into slave ships bound for America. Many would die in the miserable conditions.

ginia, in October 1859 put a bloody punctuation mark on the decade and clearly revealed the deep divisions within the country.

The presidential election of 1860 cut the last fragile bonds of union between North and South. Four men ran for the presidency in a crucial election that split the dominant Democratic Party on the issue of slavery and doomed its chances of winning.

Victory instead went to the antislavery Republican Party and its candidate, an Illinois politician named Abraham Lincoln.

Chapter 1

The Man from Illinois

Abraham Lincoln's election as president of the United States in 1860 capped one of the most amazing rises to power in American history. Just six years earlier, in 1854, the tall, gangly lawyer from Springfield, Illinois, had returned to politics from a five-year, self-imposed retirement. Since then, his only foray into the political arena was in 1858, when he lost to Stephen A. Douglas in the Illinois senatorial race.

Lincoln's presidential triumph was even more remarkable when measured against his background. Politically, his only important victory came in 1846, when he was elected for a single term to the U.S. Congress. He was not a war hero or a well-known business tycoon. He had neither wealth, power, nor influence. Nevertheless, in November 1860, Abraham Lincoln was elected the sixteenth president of the United States—the first member of the Republican Party to hold the nation's highest office. For Lincoln, the road to the White House was the quintessential American success story of a hometown boy making good.

Abraham Lincoln was born in a one-room log cabin near Hodgenville, Kentucky, on February 12, 1809, and named after his grandfather. His parents were

The log cabin in which Abraham Lincoln was born is on display at a museum near Hodgenville, Kentucky.

Thomas Lincoln and Nancy Hanks Lincoln, both transplanted Virginians. Always seeking a better life, his father moved the family several times during Lincoln's youth.

When Lincoln was nine years old and the family was living in Indiana, his mother died of "milk sickness," a disease that came from drinking the milk of cows that had eaten the poisonous white snakeroot plant. The following year his father married Sarah Bush Johnston, of whom Lincoln became quite fond.

However, he did not have those same feelings for his father. Lincoln's cousin Dennis Hanks, who lived with the family for a time, said that he doubted whether "Abe Loved his father very well or Not."[3] Apparently, the feeling was mutual; another observer of the Lincoln household noted that Thomas Lincoln never showed much respect or feeling for his son, and he seemed to think more of stepson John D. Johnston than he did of Abraham.

Some of the problems between father and son stemmed from young Lincoln's affinity for education over physical labor. In *The Inner World of Abraham Lincoln*, author Michael Burlingame writes that Thomas Lincoln used to hide, and sometimes even throw away, his son's ever-present books. Several years after Lincoln had left home for good, his father said to a friend, "I suppose that Abe is still fooling hisself with eddication. I tried to stop it, but he has got that fool idea in his head, and it can't be got out."[4] Another

thing that poisoned the relationship between the two was that his father made Lincoln turn over to him any money that he earned.

After Lincoln left home at age twenty-two, he seldom saw his father. The two were so estranged that Lincoln even refused to return home when his father was dying in 1851, telling his stepbrother that "if we could meet now, it is doubtful whether it would not be more painful than pleasant."[5] Lincoln did not attend his father's funeral.

Sensitive to Injustice

Some experts feel that these family problems are what made Lincoln sympathetic to the plight of slaves. As Burlingame wrote,

> Lincoln's deep aversion to the way his father treated him made him sensitive to the injustice suffered by slaves, with whom he probably felt a bond of identity. Just as slave owners robbed their bondsmen of the fruits of their labor, thwarted their attempts to gain an education, and abused them physically, so too did Thomas Lincoln rob Abraham of the fruits of his labor, hinder his efforts to educate himself, and occasionally beat him for no good reason.[6]

Lincoln's intense dislike of slavery may also be attributed to several trips he was hired to take aboard a flatboat to New Orleans to sell merchant's produce and other merchandise when he was about twenty. By this time Lincoln had grown into a strapping man 6'4" in height and weighing more than 200 pounds. Maneuvering the heavy flatboat with its bulky cargo along the treacherous Mississippi River was a task for which the powerful Lincoln was well suited.

Once in New Orleans, Lincoln saw the evil of slavery up close for the first time in his life. Although he was familiar with slavery, never had he seen it from this perspective: men and women in chains, waiting to be auctioned like cattle to the highest bidder;

hysterical children being torn from their parents' frantic grasp as families were broken up and sold; and the whole horrible spectacle orchestrated to the tune of the slave master's whip. According to Lincoln's cousin John Hanks, who accompanied him to New Orleans in 1831, "it was on this trip that he formed his opinions of slavery: it ran its iron in him then & there."[7]

Slaves are sold at auction as an overseer stands by with a whip. Blacks were forced to endure being sold and separated from their families.

Lincoln never forgot the cruelty of the slave marts. Two decades later, when he was a lawyer in Springfield, Illinois, a young man told him how he had become an abolitionist when he saw how slaves were mistreated in St. Louis. Referring to his New Orleans experience, Lincoln replied, "I saw it all myself when I was only a little older than you are now, and the horrid pictures are in my mind yet."[8]

Lincoln's antislavery feelings remained a strong, guiding influence throughout his entire life. "If slavery is not wrong, nothing is wrong," he wrote in 1864. "I cannot remember when I did not so think, and feel."[9]

In February 1830, Lincoln reached the age of twenty-one, which legally freed him from any obligation to turn over money he earned to his father. In the spring of 1831, after helping his family move yet again—to a spot on the Sangamon River near Decatur, Illinois—Lincoln left home for good.

A Clerk, Politician, and Soldier

Initially, he settled in the town of New Salem, Illinois, where he got a job as a store clerk. His thirst for education, along with the ability to tell a good story, made him a local favorite. In March 1832, he entered politics, running for the lower house of the state legislature. He also enlisted to fight in the Black Hawk War; later he would joke that, although he did not see combat, he fought many battles against mosquitoes.

Lincoln lost his first political campaign, finishing eighth in a field of thirteen candidates. Although the defeat left him feeling adrift in the world, he quickly righted himself. Before long he was a surveyor, rail-splitter, and farmhand, and also served as the New Salem postmaster.

During his first campaign, Lincoln quipped that if he lost, he would run five or six more times before quitting politics for good. True to his word, Lincoln again ran for the Illinois state legislature in 1834. This time he won, the first of four straight victories to the legislature. Of the two major political parties (Democrat and Whig), Lincoln's views were more in harmony with the Whigs, and he soon became an important member of the Illinois Whig Party.

The Whig Party

Although it was one of the dominant political parties in the United States for two decades, the Whig Party was never more than a collection of individuals and groups opposed to Democratic Party policies. The Whigs formed in the early 1830s, and by 1840 they were strong enough to elect their first president, William Henry Harrison. His death, after just one month in office, was a foreshadowing of things to come for the Whigs. (The party's other successful presidential candidate, Zachary Taylor, also died in office.)

Virtually from the party's birth, the Whigs were torn between the antislavery "Conscience" Whigs and the pro-Southern "Cotton" Whigs. Even though two of America's leading political figures were Whigs–Henry Clay and Daniel Webster–the party couldn't stop itself from disintegrating over slavery after the presidential election of 1852. The Conscience Whigs joined the new Republican Party, while the Cotton Whigs merged with the Democrats.

Lincoln quickly gained a reputation as a quick-witted, sharp-tongued politician. During a reply to a Democratic legislator who had criticized him, and who lived in a house with a prominent lightning rod, Lincoln said, "I would rather die . . . than feel compelled to erect a lightning rod to protect a guilty conscience from an offended God."[10] He became so skilled at verbally skewering the opposing party that a newspaper observed, "A girl might be born and become a mother before the Van Buren men [Democrats] will forget Mr. Lincoln."[11]

Taking a Stand on Slavery

It was in the Illinois legislature that Lincoln first publicly revealed his feelings toward slavery. In 1837, during his second term, the legislature overwhelmingly passed a resolution condemning abolitionists (those who wanted to abolish slavery). Just two members—Lincoln and Dan Stone—protested against the measure, calling slavery both an injustice and a bad policy.

In general, however, early in his political career, Lincoln indirectly expressed his feelings about slavery. Once, in 1837, while riding a train, Lincoln was talking to a group of men when one asked him if he was an abolitionist. Lincoln leaned over, put his hand on the shoulder of another man in the group who was a well-known abolitionist, and said, "I am mighty near one."[12]

While serving in the legislature, Lincoln also studied law. In the autumn of 1836 he was licensed to practice law in Illinois, and the following year he became a partner in the firm of his friend John Todd Stuart. In 1844 he began his own law firm in Springfield with William H. Herndon, who became a lifelong friend.

As a lawyer, Lincoln utilized the same skills he used in politics: a quick mind, a sharp phrase, and, especially, humor. He seemed to have a funny story for every situation; when he told one, he used his talent for mimicry to assume the role of each character in the story, making the humor that much sharper. As Herndon noted, when Lincoln told a story,

> All his features seemed to take part in the performance. As he neared the pith or point of the joke or story every vestige of seriousness disappeared from his face. His little gray eyes sparkled; a smile seemed to gather up, curtain-like, the corners of his mouth; his frame quivered with suppressed excitement; and when the point or "nub" of the story,—as he called it—came, no one's laugh was heartier than his.[13]

But although he enjoyed the law, Lincoln's first love was politics. It is uncertain why he declined to run for a fifth term in the Illinois state legislature in 1842, but some believed that he wanted to run for the U.S. Congress. Around this time, Lincoln wrote to a friend about his political ambitions, asking him to make sure that people knew that he wanted to go to Congress.

Abraham Lincoln as a young lawyer. Although he enjoyed practicing law, Lincoln's first love was politics.

Although he did not receive the Whig Party nomination for Congress that year, Lincoln continued to seek the opportunity to run. The problem for the Whigs was that Illinois was dominated by the Democratic Party. The few offices that Whigs could hope to win were hotly contested, and Lincoln was just one of many politicians fighting for these favored seats.

One staunchly pro-Whig area was Illinois's Seventh Congressional District. Three men—Lincoln, Edward D. Baker, and John J. Hardin—contended for the Whig congressional nomination for this district. Ultimately, a unique arrangement was reached: Each man would run for single, consecutive terms, beginning with Hardin and followed by Baker and Lincoln.

In 1846, when his turn came, Lincoln was elected to Congress, defeating Peter Cartwright, the Democratic candidate, by approximately fifteen hundred votes (6,340 to 4,829). According to one story, Lincoln's friends raised $200 for his campaign. After the election he returned $199.25, claiming to have spent just 75 cents.

Even though he finally won the office he had long coveted, Lincoln felt strangely unsatisfied. He wrote to his friend Joshua Speed that his election was not as pleasurable as he had anticipated. Perhaps this was because he knew it would be for only one term, because of the arrangement made with other Whigs.

Another factor that dampened Lincoln's enthusiasm for Congress was the existing political situation. Although he had hoped that the Whigs would pursue an agenda of domestic improvements, such as building roads and bridges and establishing schools, the party was preoccupied with opposing the war then being fought between the United States and Mexico. Domestic politics were lost in the heated rhetoric between the parties, as the Whigs blamed the Democrats for starting the war and the Democrats fought back.

As a dutiful Whig, Lincoln toed the party line, claiming in one speech that the war was both unnecessary and unconstitutional. He also criticized Democratic president James K. Polk, calling him "a bewildered, confounded and miserably perplexed man."[14]

Rising Above Party Politics

Overall, Lincoln's sole term in Congress was undistinguished. However, in January 1849 he rose above partisan politics by introducing a resolution to abolish slavery in the District of Columbia. The resolution freed all children born to slave mothers in the district after January 1, 1850, and called for them to be educated and supported by the owners of their mothers. It also banned new slaves from being brought into the district.

Perhaps to make it more palatable to slavery supporters, Lincoln tempered this controversial proposal by adding a proviso that required authorities in Washington, D.C., to arrest all fugitive slaves and return them to their owners. The resolution stopped short of abolishing slavery in the district, reflecting Lincoln's belief that Congress did not have the right to interfere with slavery where it already existed. Instead, the resolution called for a special election so that Washington, D.C., voters could decide for themselves whether they supported emancipation.

The resolution provoked a fiery debate between pro- and antislavery forces on the floor of the House of Representatives, a debate in which Lincoln, surprisingly, did not participate. The resolution was defeated.

On March 3, 1849, Lincoln's congressional term expired, and he returned to Springfield. Although he campaigned vigorously for General Zachary Taylor, the successful Whig candidate for president in 1848, Lincoln did not receive the prestigious federal job that he desired in return (commissioner of the General Land Office). This failure haunted Lincoln; he felt that his political career was over.

For the next five years (1849–1854), with his political ambitions thwarted, Lincoln concentrated on his law practice and domestic life. He was a very tall, very lean man with rumpled black hair, sideburns running down almost to the bottom of his ears, and a reputation for careless grooming; his vest was usually wrinkled, and his pants often crept up his leg past the ankle.

In 1842 Lincoln had married Mary Todd, a small, plump woman prone to fits of temper. Keen on advancing in society, she tried to remove some of her husband's rough frontier edges, but she couldn't break him of such habits as answering the front door in his carpet slippers and shirt sleeves or lying on his back on the floor and reading. His casual manner sometimes embarrassed her. Once, when two society women called for

15

Mary Todd Lincoln

Few women have been more miserable in the White House than Mary Todd Lincoln, who ironically had always yearned to be the wife of a president.

Born in Lexington, Kentucky, in 1818, to a slaveholding family, she moved to Springfield, Illinois, in 1839, where she met Abraham Lincoln, a struggling young lawyer and politician. Although she had once said she would marry only a man who would become president, she married Lincoln on November 4, 1842, when his chances of gaining the presidency were remote. Yet as time proved, Lincoln was indeed elected president, and the couple moved into the White House in 1861.

There, unfortunately, Mary found only misery. Because of the war, there were few social functions at which she could entertain, and the death of her son Willie in 1862 made her bitter, angry, and depressed. Her anxiety was further increased by the fact that four of her brothers fought for the Confederacy, and one was killed. With Lincoln's reelection and the end of the war, Mary hoped for better days, but the assassination of her husband in April 1865 put an end to those dreams. Her last years were marred by mental illness and a vicious fight with her son Robert, who succeeded in placing her in a sanitarium for one year. She died in 1882.

Mary Todd's life in the White House was a miserable one.

Mary, Lincoln answered the door and invited them inside, explaining that his wife would "be down soon as she gets her trotting harness on."[15]

But despite their sometimes rocky marriage, the Lincolns remained together, and their family grew. Their first son, Robert Todd Lincoln, was born in 1843. He was followed by Edward in 1846, William in 1850, and Thomas (Tad), born in 1853.

During the five years after he left Congress, Lincoln essentially retired from public life. Although he made speeches for Whig candidates and spoke at the eulogies of Whig heroes such as Henry Clay and Zachary Taylor, Lincoln was not involved in the party's daily activities. He seemed content occupying his time with his growing family and burgeoning law practice, but he was dismayed that politics, once such a vital part of his life, had apparently turned its back on him. As Herndon wrote, "[He] despaired of ever rising again in the political world."[16]

Mexico—applied to be admitted to the Union as a free state. In a replay of the Missouri crisis, pro- and antislavery forces battled over the balance of power and the extension or confinement of slavery, while California's statehood hung in the balance.

Each time a solution was offered (extend the Missouri Compromise line to the Pacific, prohibit slavery in all territories, deny the power of Congress to prohibit slavery, or let the citizens of each territory exercise popular sovereignty), one side or the other found it unacceptable. As in 1820, slavery brought the country to the brink of anarchy.

Finally, Henry Clay, proving that he was indeed the "Great Pacificator," once again fashioned a compromise to end another debilitating national crisis over slavery. Clay's Compromise of 1850 was a series of five legislature measures designed to appease both pro- and anti-slavery forces. For slavery opponents, California was admitted into the Union as a free state, and the slave trade (but not slavery itself) was abolished in the District of Columbia. For slavery supporters, the remaining territories won from Mexico, which were named New Mexico (now the states of New Mexico and Arizona) and Utah,

were granted popular sovereignty. Another measure awarded Texas $10 million for territorial claims.

The Fugitive Slave Law

By far the most controversial part of the Compromise of 1850 was the enactment of a new Fugitive Slave Law. A significant concession to the South, this harsh law was aimed at halting the Underground Railroad. It enabled any master or master's agent to claim that any black anywhere in the country was a fugitive slave, without having to offer further proof. The alleged fugitive was immediately arrested and returned to his or her supposed master. Blacks were forbidden to

This cartoon from 1851 depicts the North and South battling over the Fugitive Slave Law. The severe law was in fact a controversial matter.

testify on their own behalf or even to have a jury trial. The law also levied a $1,000 fine and six months in prison for anyone found helping a fugitive slave.

The North exploded with outrage over this unfair law. Because of it, no black anywhere was safe from slavery. The long arm of the South's peculiar institution could enter any community in any state and drag a black person back into slavery merely on the word of a master.

Suddenly and frighteningly at risk, thousands of blacks fled to Canada; the black population of Ontario doubled to eleven thousand during the 1850s. Others armed themselves, determined to fight and die if necessary rather than be returned to slavery.

Abolitionists, formerly advocates of nonviolence, also began reaching for guns, taking to heart Frederick Douglass's advice: "The only way to make the Fugitive Slave Law a dead letter is to make half a dozen or more dead kidnappers."[40] Boston, in particular, seethed with abolitionist anger over the law. After it required more than five hundred armed men to return one alleged fugitive slave, masters and their agents avoided Boston. Violence and bloodshed broke out in numerous communities throughout the North, as abolitionists and blacks fought masters and their agents.

While it was obvious to many that the Compromise of 1850 would not hold—Pennsylvania senator Thaddeus Stevens predicted that it would bring civil war—others felt differently. The woefully out-of-touch

president, Millard Fillmore, said that the compromise was a "final settlement of the dangerous and exciting subjects which they embraced," while Michigan senator Lewis Cass confidently said that "the question [slavery] is settled in the public mind."[41]

But it was not settled, as the violence and defiance toward the Fugitive Slave Law clearly proved. The publication of Harriet Beecher Stowe's antislavery novel *Uncle Tom's Cabin* in 1852 further aroused feelings in the North against slavery and feelings in the South against abolitionists.

It was against this incendiary background that Illinois senator Stephen A. Douglas introduced his Kansas-Nebraska bill early in 1854. Because of the new concessions awarded to the South by the Kansas-Nebraska Act, particularly the repeal of the 36° 30' latitudinal ban on slavery, many Northerners felt that no compromise would ever be sufficient for slaveholders. No matter what the North gave up, the South would want more.

"You may pass it [the Kansas-Nebraska bill] here," said Ohio senator Salmon P. Chase. "You may send it to the other House. It may become law. But its effect will be to satisfy all thinking men that no compromise[s] with slavery will endure, except so long as they serve the interests of slavery."[42]

Kansas-Nebraska Act Passes

Despite fierce opposition, Congress eventually passed the Kansas-Nebraska Act. Soon, pro- and antislavery settlers were battling

Although Lincoln may have missed public life, being out of politics was one of the best things that ever happened to him. During that time he underwent a profound metamorphosis, changing from a partisan politician to a man of vision.

Lincoln experts agree that these five years altered him forever, and for the better. Albert J. Beveridge called them years "of waiting, thought and growth," and felt that during this time Lincoln replaced "narrow partisanship and small purposes" with the "foundations of greatness."[17]

Lincoln apparently spent the years from 1849 to 1854 coming to terms with his "failures," as he saw them, and charting the future course of his life. Michael Burlingame, in *The Inner World of Abraham Lincoln*, wrote, "Between 1849 and 1854, Lincoln seems to have worked hard on this task of healing the wounds of ego deflation and thus prepared himself well for leaving behind a legacy that, as it turned out, was monumental indeed."[18]

To Lincoln, leaving a legacy was important. His friend Joshua Speed recalled his speaking about it:

> He said to me that he had done nothing to make any human being remember that he had lived—and that to connect his name with the events transpiring in his day & generation and so impress himself upon them, as to link his name with something that would redound to the interest of his fellow man was what he desired to live for.[19]

One issue that Lincoln contemplated at length during his five years out of politics was slavery. In 1850, his friend John T. Stuart remarked that the time was rapidly approaching when all men would have to choose between abolitionism and the pro-slavery Democratic Party. Lincoln firmly replied that his mind was made up; slavery could not be compromised. As it turned out, it was slavery that led to Lincoln's return to politics—and, ultimately, to the presidency.

The Kansas-Nebraska Act

Early in 1854, the United States was rocked by a furious debate over the controversial Kansas-Nebraska Act. Sponsored by Democratic senator Stephen A. Douglas from Illinois, the bill created the territories of Nebraska and Kansas to the west of Missouri and Iowa. The act's hidden purpose was to facilitate construction of a transcontinental railroad along a northern route (rather than along a more southerly route) that would benefit both Douglas and Illinois.

To gain Southern support for the bill, however, Douglas agreed to repeal a key provision of the Missouri Compromise that prohibited slavery in territories north of the $36°$ $30'$ line of latitude. Instead, the Kansas-Nebraska Act enabled the inhabitants of each territory to decide whether or not they wanted slavery, a concept known as "popular sovereignty."

"If the people of Kansas want a slaveholding state," said Douglas, "let them have it, and if they want a free state they have a

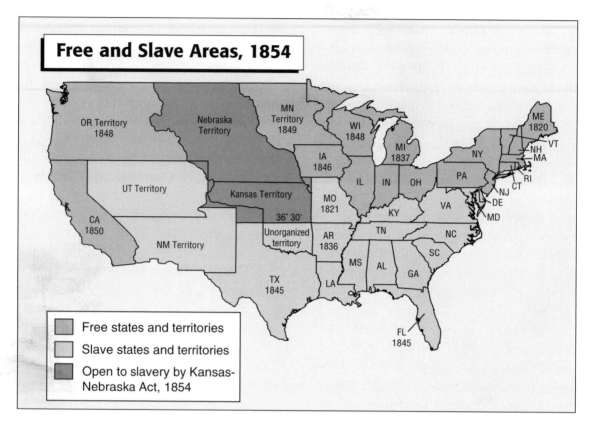

Free and Slave Areas, 1854

OR Territory 1848

Nebraska Territory

MN Territory 1849

WI 1848

ME 1820

VT

NH

MA

NY

UT Territory

Kansas Territory

IA 1846

MI 1837

PA

RI

CT

IL IN OH

NJ

DE

CA 1850

36° 30'

MO 1821

KY

VA

MD

NM Territory

Unorganized territory

AR 1836

TN

NC

TX 1845

LA

MS AL GA

SC

FL 1845

Free states and territories

Slave states and territories

Open to slavery by Kansas-Nebraska Act, 1854

right to it, and it is not for the people of Illinois, or Missouri, or New York, or Kentucky, to complain, whatever the decision of the people of Kansas may be."[20]

The possible repeal of 36° 30' unleashed a firestorm of protest in the North. Suddenly, the long-held hopes of antislavery proponents that slavery would eventually wither and die thanks to the 36° 30' barrier were wiped away. The Kansas-Nebraska Act seemed to breathe new life into slavery and offer it unlimited potential for growth in the vast territorial lands that were not yet states. In New England, 3,050 clergymen signed a letter to

the U.S. Senate protesting the passage of the Kansas-Nebraska Act in the name of God; 500 more ministers did the same in the Northwest. In Chicago, a hostile crowd of 8,000 repeatedly interrupted Douglas with boos, groans, catcalls, and hisses as he tried to speak and defend his controversial law.

And in Springfield, the slumbering politician within Abraham Lincoln was jolted awake by the repeal of 36° 30'. Aroused as never before by the prospect of slavery's spreading into the territories, Lincoln went on the offensive. He spoke out against slavery at every opportunity,

Abraham Lincoln takes to the podium during one of his debates with Stephen Douglas, who is standing behind him. There were seven debates in all.

in his arguments against slavery. The famous document was the wellspring of Lincoln's political philosophy: "I have never had a feeling politically that did not spring from the sentiments embodied in the Declaration,"[27] he once said.)

Because of the notoriety of Lincoln and Douglas, and the important issues they were debating, the campaign took on a national scope. The debates were the first political speeches ever recorded in shorthand by newspaper correspondents, who accompanied the candidates on the campaign trail. Because of this, the speeches were reprinted almost verbatim in newspapers across the country. People in every part of the nation could read precisely what each man said and draw their own conclusions about slavery.

Ultimately, Lincoln lost the election. Although he received 4,085 more votes than Douglas, the Democrats gained control of the Illinois legislature; under the system then in effect, the legislature named the U.S. senator. When the Illinois legislature met in January 1859, they elected Douglas as senator by a vote of fifty-four to forty-six.

Although he lost, Lincoln was glad to have had the opportunity to run. "Though I now sink out of view, and shall be forgotten, I believe I have made some marks which will tell for the cause of civil liberty long after I am gone,"[28] he said.

He couldn't have been more wrong. Rather than "sink out of view," Lincoln was about to be elevated to the American equivalent of political royalty: the presidency of the United States. It would happen in the watershed year of 1860, when politics, slavery, and secession would combine to make it the most important year in the brief history of the United States of America.

Chapter 2

The South and Slavery

The election of 1860 was a milestone for the United States. For the first time, voters were offered a clear choice about the country's most important social, economic, and political issue: slavery. Ever since the War for Independence, slavery had polarized American society; by 1860 it could no longer be compromised, negotiated, or ignored. The road to the critical 1860 election was littered with previously unsuccessful efforts to resolve this volatile and divisive issue.

Attempts to establish a compromise on slavery that would satisfy both pro- and antislavery forces in the United States began soon after the colonies won their independence from Great Britain. An estimated five thousand blacks had fought for America during the war. In New England, blacks were key members of the militia. Their invalu-able contributions to the war effort helped many Northerners realize the contradiction in claiming to be fighting a war for human freedom while one segment of the

Blacks fought in the War for Independence. Here, a black militiaman shoots a British major at the Battle of Lexington.

population was enslaved. Beginning in 1780, the Northern states of Pennsylvania, Massachusetts, Connecticut, Rhode Island, New York, and New Jersey moved to outlaw slavery.

The Northwest Ordinance

After the war, blacks who had fought with the American army were given free land in the western United States as a reward, just as other soldiers were. In 1787, Congress, operating under the Articles of Confederation, passed the Northwest Ordinance. This prohibited slavery in the lands west of the Appalachian Mountains, north of the Ohio River, and east of the Mississippi River.

However, the Articles of Confederation did not provide a strong foundation on which to build a new country. In the summer of 1787, the Constitutional Convention met in Philadelphia to design a new framework to govern the United States.

It didn't take long for slavery to cause problems at the convention. Because issues like taxation and the number of congressmen allotted per state were linked to each state's population, a debate ensued over whether slaves counted as inhabitants or were just "property." Gouverneur Morris of Pennsylvania asked the delegates if slaves were to be considered as men or property. If they were men, he said, they should be made citizens and allowed to vote.

The stakes riding on the answer to this question were high. If slaves counted as inhabitants, then states like South Carolina and Georgia, which had large slave populations, would have more congressional representatives, and thus more political power. Therefore Northern delegates argued that slaves were property, while Southerners claimed they were inhabitants.

The issue threatened to deadlock the convention until a compromise was reached. It was decided that, for purposes of population, each slave would be counted as three-fifths of a person. Thus every five slaves equaled three free men.

No sooner was that issue settled than another argument occurred concerning the slave trade—bringing slaves into the country from Africa. Northern delegates wanted this practice abolished, while Southerners demanded that it continue. Finally, another compromise was reached that continued the slave trade until 1808.

(Curiously, another pro-slavery provision included in the Constitution, which required fugitive slaves to be returned to their owners, generated little opposition. According to Roger Sherman of Connecticut, that clause was as logical as one that made it a crime to steal a horse.)

Slavery continued to haunt the convention, threatening at any moment to bring it to a halt. When the Pennsylvania Antislavery Society gave Benjamin Franklin a resolution urging him to call for slavery's abolition, he pocketed the document rather than risk his colleagues' wrath by bringing the matter up for debate. When the Constitution was finished and sent to the states for ratification, the compromises

The compromises made by the members of the Constitutional Convention (pictured) would eventually lead to the Civil War nearly seventy-five years later.

on slavery were evident. Some who opposed slavery were concerned that the Constitution did not abolish the practice. Thomas Jefferson, himself a slaveholder, called slavery an abomination and said that it was like holding a wolf by the ears; you didn't like it, but you didn't dare let it go. "Nothing is more certainly written in the book of fate than that these people are to be free,"[29] said Jefferson.

In general, however, it was felt that the inherent and obvious immorality of slavery would inevitably lead to its demise in a nation based on individual liberty and human freedom. The contradiction between a country that claimed all men were created equal and at the same time allowed one race to be subjugated by an-

other was too great for slavery to survive. The compromises in the Constitution were considered temporary measures to prevent the issue from derailing the convention. In reality, however, these compromises were just the first in a series of wrong assumptions and political miscalculations about slavery that would ultimately lead to the Civil War.

The first inkling that slavery was not going to fade away merely because of lofty platitudes came in 1808. That year, as per

Eli Whitney and the Cotton Gin

Ironically, it was Northerner Eli Whitney and his invention of the cotton gin that helped slavery become firmly entrenched in the South.

Born in Massachusetts in 1765, Whitney was a guest at the Georgia plantation of Catharine Greene in 1792 when he designed and built his first cotton gin. The machine consisted of sawlike teeth attached to a cylinder. When the cylinder was turned, the teeth passed through the ribs of a fixed comb. As the cotton was fed into the machine, the fibers were pulled through, but the seeds were prevented from going through by the ribs.

Almost overnight, a process that had been long and tedious when done manually became quick and economical when performed by machine. It had taken one slave ten hours to produce a pound of cotton lint; the cotton gin could produce three hundred to one thousand pounds of lint per day. Cotton went from a seldom-planted crop to the most important in the South. As more cotton was planted, more slaves were needed to pick it, and thus slavery became a vital cog in the South's economic engine.

Whitney never profited from the cotton gin, because a factory fire curtailed his ability to make the machine and because others copied

By making cotton much easier to process, the cotton gin was an important factor in the spread of slavery in the South.

his design. He subsequently developed the mass-production system of standardized parts. Whitney died in Connecticut in 1825.

the constitutional compromise, Congress ended the slave trade by passing a law forbidding the importation of slaves into any port in the country. However, the law was halfheartedly enforced in the South; slavery not only continued, but prospered. To get around the law, some people began raising slaves, like a farmer raises crops, to supply the growing demand for

captive labor without having to import it into the country.

The reason why slaves were suddenly in such demand that laws were ignored was that this was a different South than the one that had agreed in 1787 to end the slave trade. Eli Whitney's 1793 invention of the cotton gin had profoundly altered the region, giving rise to an entirely new economy based solely on cotton. In 1776, only 1 million pounds of cotton had been grown in the South; by 1809, the total was 86 million pounds and increasing rapidly.

A Slave-Based Economy

This new Southern economy, which made many large plantation owners wealthy, was totally dependent on slaves' performing the backbreaking chore of picking cotton. Thus in the South, antislavery sentiment, which had been present after the American Revolution just as it had been in the North, faded under the lure of riches promised by the cotton economy.

As the South became more dependent on slavery, it began to rationalize dependence on it. The concept of slavery was twisted until it was presented as a benefit for blacks. Otherwise reasonable men and women convinced themselves that blacks were not as intelligent as whites, and thus would be unable to survive without slavery's caring for them. Using this "logic," Southerners actually convinced themselves that blacks enjoyed living in bondage.

"If only the abolitionists could see how happy our people are," said slave owner Hiram B. Tibbetts in 1848. "The idea of unhappiness would never en-

ter the mind of any one witnessing their enjoyments."[30]

Others placed slavery in a historical context to try and justify its existence. "There is not a respectable system of civilization known to history whose foundations were not laid in the institution of domestic slavery,"[31] said Virginia senator Robert M. T. Hunter.

South Carolina senator John C. Calhoun, a vociferous defender of the Southern way of life, said that slavery was good and that those who had once called it a moral and political evil didn't believe so any more.

By theorizing that blacks were unable to survive in America, many Southerners convinced themselves that slaves enjoyed living in bondage.

Opposition to slavery primarily came from abolitionist societies. In the early years of the nineteenth century, these groups were badly organized, poorly financed, and generally ineffective. As their reason for ending slavery, they used the same arguments about freedom and liberty that had compelled the colonists to fight against the British. Often these societies printed newspapers promoting their views, which didn't enjoy much circulation and vanished after only a few issues. Although the abolitionists were sincere, they were extremely benign in their approach, hoping that high-minded statements about the immorality of slavery would convince people to end it. To those who were growing rich from slave labor, these arguments had little impact.

By 1818, pro-slavery and antislavery forces in the United States had reached an uneasy equilibrium; there were eleven slave states and eleven free states in the country. Neither side felt that the other had an advantage. Then, in 1818, Missouri, part of the Louisiana Purchase territory, applied for admission to the Union as a slaveholding state. Determined to keep the balance of political power from shifting to the South, New York congressman James Tallmadge introduced an amendment to the statehood bill that prohibited any further importation of slaves into Missouri. It also freed the children of Missouri slaves when they reached age twenty-five. The amendment was never passed.

The bill successfully passed the House of Representatives, which had a majority of representatives from the more populous free states, but ran into a roadblock in the Senate, which was more pro-Southern. The debate raged not only in the Senate chambers but throughout the country. It was feared that if Missouri were allowed to join the United States as a slave state, slavery would spread into the rest of the vast territory obtained in the Louisiana Purchase.

The Missouri Compromise

When the Senate defeated the bill for Missouri statehood, it seemed as if Congress was hopelessly deadlocked on the matter. Then Kentuckian Henry Clay, speaker of the house, devised what became known as the Missouri Compromise. It allowed Missouri to enter the Union as a slave state and Maine, which had applied for statehood in 1819, to enter as a free state, thus keeping the balance of power intact between both sides. The compromise also split the Louisiana Purchase territory into zones: Slavery was prohibited in territories north of latitude 36° 30', which was Missouri's southern boundary, but was permitted in territories below that latitude. Although Southern legislators raised concerns about putting any limits on slavery's expansion, Clay shepherded the Missouri Compromise to passage.

While some hailed the Missouri Compromise as a sound solution to the slavery

Henry Clay

Although he was one of the most influential political figures of his era, Clay never attained the prize he wanted most—the presidency—despite running three times for the office.

Born in Virginia in 1777, Clay moved to Lexington, Kentucky, in 1797 and opened a law practice. While still in his twenties, he was elected to the state legislature, and from there he moved to Congress as a member of the House of Representatives. He later became a U.S. senator.

Clay's great genius was for finding a political middle ground when compromise seemed impossible. He fashioned the Missouri Compromise and the Compromise of 1850, both of which appeased anti- and pro-slavery forces. He also developed a compromise tariff that mollified South Carolina during the "nullification crisis" of 1833, when the state threatened to secede from the Union.

Clay was a nationally respected political figure, but his three attempts for the presidency failed. He became a leader of the Whig Party, but even his great negotiating skills could not stop the party from splintering over slavery. Clay died in 1852.

Henry Clay fashioned the Missouri Compromise and the Compromise of 1850.

deadlock that had threatened to paralyze the nation, others saw more ominous portents in the great debate and ultimate agreement. Thomas Jefferson worried that the matter foreshadowed the eventual destruction of the United States. "This momentous question, like a firebell in the night, awakened me and filled me with terror," he wrote. "I considered it at once the [death] knell of the Union." The problem, Jefferson added, was that the debates had established a geopolitical division in the country between North and South that could never be erased. "Every new irritation will mark it deeper and deeper,"[32] he said.

John Quincy Adams, soon to become the nation's sixth president, also saw seeds of disaster sown by the Missouri Compromise, calling it a "title-page to a great, tragic volume."[33]

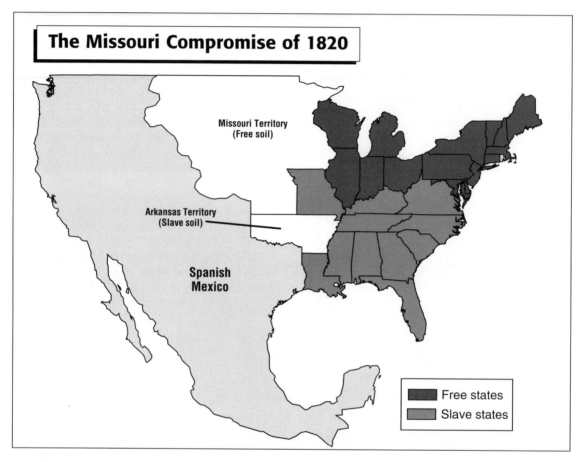

The Missouri Compromise of 1820

Missouri Territory
(Free soil)

Arkansas Territory
(Slave soil)

Spanish
Mexico

■ Free states
■ Slave states

Many Southerners saw in the passion of the antislavery speeches resulting from the Missouri Compromise the depth of Northern feeling to abolish a practice they considered essential. "The Missouri question," said John Geddes, South Carolina governor, "has given rise to the expression of opinions and doctrines respecting this specie of property, which tend not only to diminish its value, but also threaten our safety."[34]

Geddes was more correct than he realized. The slavery debates caused by the Missouri crisis reenergized the abolitionist movement in the North. General appeals to the goodness of human nature to abolish slavery were replaced by more radical and warlike calls to action. One of the first was issued in 1829 by David Walker, a free black born in North Carolina who was living in Boston. His pamphlet, entitled *Appeal to the Colored Citizens of the World,* did not couch antislavery sentiments in lofty principles but, rather, in harsh tones that called for slaves to rise against their masters and to kill or be killed:

I speak, Americans, for your good. We must and shall be free, I say, in spite of you. You may do your best to keep us in wretchedness and misery, to enrich you and your children; but God will deliver us from under you. And woe, woe, will be to you if we have to obtain our freedom by fighting.[35]

Walker's words ignited passions across the country. In the North, the abolitionist movement took on a new urgency, sparked by men like William Lloyd Garrison, who began publishing his famous antislavery newspaper the *Liberator* on January 1, 1831. "I will be as harsh as truth, and as uncompromising as justice," Garrison wrote. "On this subject I do not wish to think, or speak, or write, with moderation. . . . I am in earnest—I will not equivocate—I will not excuse—I will not retreat a single inch—and I will be heard!"[36]

For Southerners, Walker's appeal for a violent slave uprising was their worst nightmare brought to life. A reward of $1,000 was offered in the South for Walker's corpse; it rose to $10,000 if he was captured and returned to the region. Georgia also offered a $5,000 reward for the trial and conviction of Garrison under its laws.

Jefferson had been right. The line drawn in the sand between North and South was getting deeper and deeper.

Throughout the 1830s and 1840s, events caused both anti- and pro-slavery forces to harden their positions, making the likelihood of future compromise all the more unlikely. In August 1831, Nat Turner led a slave revolt in Virginia that killed sixty whites and more than one hundred blacks.

The following year, John C. Calhoun of South Carolina led a Southern planters' rebellion that was, on the surface, a protest against federal tariff laws. At its core, however, the dispute centered on the growing feeling against slavery that was spreading throughout the rest of the Union.

The tariff, as Calhoun admitted, was

but . . . the occasion, rather than the real cause of the present unhappy state of things. The truth can no longer be disguised, that the peculiar domestick [*sic*] institutions of the Southern States, and the consequent direction which that and her soil and climate have given to her industry, has placed them in regard to taxation and appropriation in opposite relation to the majority of the Union.[37]

Bold action by President Andrew Jackson, including threats to hang the leaders of the tariff rebellion, led to its collapse. "The Union must be preserved at all hazards and any price," Jackson said to South Carolina. "Disunion by armed force is treason."[38] But although it backed down this time, through its belligerency South Carolina had demonstrated that it would not idly submit to the federal government when its "peculiar domestic institutions" were threatened.

As slavery became more entrenched in the South, abolitionists fought back by instituting the Underground Railroad to help runaway slaves flee to freedom in the North or Canada. Abolitionist organizations, such as the American Anti-Slavery Society, grew in membership, strength, and influence.

For almost thirty years, the Missouri Compromise kept slavery from tearing apart the Union. Then, near the end of the 1840s, another national crisis erupted over slavery. As with Missouri, this one also was caused by America's expanding borders.

The Wilmot Proviso

On August 8, 1846, during the Mexican War, Democratic congressman David Wilmot of Pennsylvania offered an amendment to an appropriations bill that would prohibit slavery in any territories obtained from Mexico as a result of the war. Not only did this amendment once again bring slavery directly into the political spotlight, but it also threatened to split the Democratic Party into anti- and pro-slavery factions as members took sides on what was known as the Wilmot Proviso.

"The slavery question . . . cannot fail to destroy the Democratic Party, if it does not ultimately threaten the Union itself,"[39] wrote President James K. Polk.

Although the Wilmot Proviso passed the House of Representatives, it failed in the Senate. But the entire country now knew that the question of what to do with any territory acquired from Mexico was

The Underground Railroad

The Underground Railroad was a network of antislavery Northerners who hid and sheltered fugitive slaves and helped them escape to freedom, either in the North or in Canada.

Although the railroad was begun by Quakers in the 1780s, it achieved notoriety beginning in the 1830s, as the slavery debate grew more intense. Traveling by night, and navigating via the North Star, fugitives would either seek stations on their own or be met by "conductors" who escorted them to safety. Harriet Tubman was one of the most famous conductors on the Underground Railroad.

The Underground Railroad was a potent weapon for Northern antislavery groups. Although a harsh Fugitive Slave Law, as part of the Compromise of 1850, was targeted directly at the railroad, it continued operating. The South's bitterness over the Underground Railroad was one of the indirect causes of the Civil War,

Conductors of the Underground Railroad hide a fugitive slave in a shipping crate.

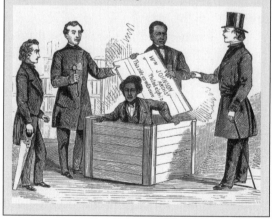

going to pit pro- and antislavery forces against each other in a bitter conflict.

The struggle began in 1849, when California—which had been obtained from

calling it a "monstrous injustice," a "vast moral evil," and a "monster."[21]

Abraham Lincoln had found the spark to reignite his political flame. Every one of the 175 speeches he gave from 1854 through 1860 was dominated by a single theme: the need to exclude slavery from the territories.

Passage of the Kansas-Nebraska Act not only further inflamed the slavery debate but dealt a fatal blow to the feeble Whig Party, which had always been hopelessly divided over the issue of slavery. Southern Whigs who opposed the law found support for both themselves and their party virtually nil in that part of the country. Meanwhile, Northern Whigs, as well as antislavery Democrats, abolitionists, Know-Nothings, and others, came together before the year was out to form a new party called the Republicans, united at first only in their opposition to the extension of slavery.

A Republican Party Leader

Lincoln continued his relentless attacks against slavery and became a leader of the new Republican Party in Illinois. In Charleston, Illinois, he vowed to continue the fight against slavery "until everywhere on this wide land, the sun shall shine and the rain shall fall and the wind shall blow upon no man who goes forth to unrequited toil."[22] He also addressed the growing talk of secession by some Southerners, proclaiming, "We will say to the Southern disunionists, *We* won't go out of the Union, and you *shan't*."[23]

James Buchanan

The fifteenth president of the United States, despite a distinguished political career, was ill prepared to deal with the growing animosity between pro- and antislavery forces during his tenure in office.

Born in Pennsylvania, Buchanan served in both houses of Congress, as minister to Russia and Great Britain, and also as secretary of state in the cabinet of President James K. Polk. During the contentious debate over the Kansas-Nebraska Act, Buchanan was minister to Great Britain, and thus he was not personally involved in the controversy. This made him the perfect choice as a Democratic presidential candidate in 1856; he defeated Republican John C. Fremont and Know-Nothing candidate Millard Fillmore.

Within a few days of Buchanan's inauguration, the Supreme Court announced its *Dred Scott* decision, and the already white-hot debate over slavery grew even hotter. As president, Buchanan attempted to steer a middle course between North and South; the result was that he satisfied neither and was considered a weak and indecisive president. After one term he left the White House and returned to Pennsylvania, where he died in 1868.

James Buchanan

In the presidential election of 1856, John C. Fremont, the Republican candidate, received 114 electoral votes and 1,341,264 popular votes—a strong showing for a new political party. (The winner,

Democrat James Buchanan, received 174 electoral votes and 1,838,169 popular votes.) After the election, the Republicans continued to gain strength in the northern and western parts of the country.

"A House Divided . . ."

Thanks to the stature Lincoln had gained from his attacks on slavery, it was a foregone conclusion that the Illinois Republicans would nominate him to run for the Senate against Stephen Douglas in 1858. When Lincoln accepted the nomination, he gave a speech whose power, clarity, and vision still resonate today. "I believe this government cannot endure, permanently half slave and half free," he said. "A house divided against itself cannot stand."[24]

When he heard that the Republicans had nominated Lincoln to run against him, Douglas knew he was in for a difficult campaign, calling Lincoln the top man in his party and the best stump speaker in the West.

The campaign was indeed a bitter one, highlighted by a series of debates in seven Illinois towns. Thousands of people turned out to watch the verbal fireworks fly between the two candidates. At the first debate in Ottawa, ten thousand people came to see the candidates, drenching the town in dust from their movements. Each street corner was festooned with banners, flags, slogans, and other political paraphernalia. To add to the carnival atmosphere, military companies and marching bands wandered up and down the street.

Douglas was as good a speaker as Lincoln. The debates were lively and sharp, with both men hurling charges and countercharges at each other. Douglas labeled the Republicans a sectional party that was dividing the country through its antislavery policies. Not only did he call Lincoln an abolitionist, but he also said that Lincoln favored racial equality, an explosive charge during an age when such a thing was considered shamefully repugnant.

Douglas left no doubt where he stood on racial equality. He explained that the founding fathers had intended the American government to be run by white men, both now and in the future. "The signers of the Declaration had no reference to the negro . . . or any other inferior and degraded race, when they spoke of the equality of men,"[25] Douglas said.

Lincoln calmly denied that he favored racial equality. He also tried to move the debate to a loftier plane:

> Let us discard all this quibbling about this man and the other man—this race and that race and the other race being inferior. [Instead, let us] unite as one people throughout this land, until we shall once more stand up declaring that all men are created equal.[26]

(It was no accident that Lincoln turned to the ideas of freedom and equality embodied in the Declaration of Independence

each other in a bloody civil war in Kansas, as each side was determined to make its view prevail when the territory applied for statehood. The term *Bleeding Kansas* became not just a nickname but an accurate representation of the savage events occurring within the territory. Clearly, popular sovereignty wasn't the answer to the slavery question either.

With both North and South aroused to a fever pitch by the Fugitive Slave Law, the repeal of the Missouri Compromise, the Kansas-Nebraska Act, and the civil war in Kansas, another slavery controversy erupted in 1857: The U.S. Supreme Court issued its decision in the *Dred Scott* case.

Dred Scott was a slave owned by an army officer who, in the 1830s, had taken Scott into Illinois and then north, into territory where slavery had been banned by the Missouri Compromise. Scott sued for his freedom based on the fact that his residence in a free territory made him a free man.

In a crushing blow to antislavery forces, the Supreme Court, under Chief Justice Roger Taney, a Southern sympathizer who yet had freed his own slaves, ruled against Scott. According to the Court's interpretation of the Constitution, blacks had been regarded by the founding fathers as being of "an inferior order," so inferior that they had "no rights which a white man was bound to respect." [43] Furthermore, the Court also ruled that, because the Constitution recognized slavery, Congress could not exclude it from the territories, and thus the Missouri Compromise was unconstitutional.

Dred Scott petititioned for his freedom in a case that went all the way to the Supreme Court. The Court ruled against him.

For many Northerners, this was the last straw. It seemed as if the Supreme Court had opened the slavery floodgates; nothing could stop it now from engulfing the entire country. Abraham Lincoln spoke for many when he asked how long it would be before the Court ruled that "the Constitution of the United States does not permit a state to exclude slavery from its limits." [44]

Because of slavery, the United States was a tinderbox, just waiting for the fuse to be lit that would cause an explosion to shatter the Union. In October 1859, a man named John Brown struck the match.

Chapter 3

Watershed Year: 1860

O n the night of October 16, 1859, a ragtag band of twenty-two armed men stormed the federal government's armory at Harpers Ferry, Virginia. With the element of surprise as their chief weapon, the group captured the armory and several other buildings. The tiny army, which included five free blacks, hoped that this attack would spark a widespread insurrection among captive blacks that would ultimately consume slavery. Instead, it just hastened the beginning of the bloodiest war in American history.

The leader of the attack was a fifty-nine-year-old ardent abolitionist named John Brown. Throughout the course of his life, he had been many things—a tanner, businessman, wool dealer, cattle breeder, and farmer—but one thing that never changed was his hatred of slavery, which began when he saw a white man beating a slave boy with a shovel. At one time, he considered operating a school for black youths, believing that education was the key to destroying slavery.

Eventually, however, Brown traded his peaceful ideas for more violent ones. Studying other slave rebellions throughout history (such as during the Roman Empire), Brown conceived a plan that was both daring and hopeless. He decided to form an army of slave liberation based in the portion of the Appalachian Mountains that stretched from Virginia to Alabama. His goal was to defeat any armed force that opposed him—including that of the U.S. government—while establishing the basis of a free Southern state. Brown was certain that once slaves heard of his existence, they would throw off their shackles by the thousands and join him. He would then use this formidable force to compel the Southern states to renounce slavery, or risk his army's wrath. "One man and God," he said, "can overturn the universe."[45]

Having fought, along with his sons, in Bleeding Kansas (where he hacked five pro-slavery advocates to death with swords), Brown was familiar with guerrilla warfare. He was a charismatic leader, a man with a flowing beard who could hold others enthralled, whether by preaching from the Bible (his favorite passage was Hebrews 9:22, "Without shedding of blood is no remission [of sin]") or merely by his presence. He was an energetic, sharp-featured man with a prominent nose and flashing dark eyes who always

John Brown (seen here before he grew a beard) hoped to inspire a slave revolt by leading a raid against the armory at Harpers Ferry.

walked with his head bent forward, as if deep in thought.

In December 1858, Brown staged a "practice" raid in Missouri. He freed eleven slaves and sent them to Canada. The following year, deciding that the time had finally come to act, Brown seized Harpers Ferry on the night of October 16 and prepared for the slave uprising that he was certain would follow. He brought with him two hundred rifles, two hundred pistols, and a thousand pikes with which to arm his slave legions. But instead of slaves, what poured into Harpers Ferry on the afternoon of October 17 were units of the Virginia militia. Brown and his followers barricaded themselves in the armory's enginehouse for a last stand.

Later that evening, a force of U.S. Marines commanded by Colonel Robert E. Lee arrived in Harpers Ferry. The next day, a Marine detachment under Lieutenant J. E. B. Stuart stormed the enginehouse. During the brief, desperate fight that followed, two of Brown's sons (Oliver and Watson) were killed, and most of the rest of his small force were either killed or wounded. Suffering from several stab wounds, Brown and four others were taken prisoner and charged with rebellion, treason, and murder.

News of Brown's raid spread through the United States like wildfire. In the initial confusion and fear, some believed that a slave rebellion had already begun. Others thought that the attack on Harpers Ferry was the first step in an abolitionist plot to

At Harpers Ferry, J. E. B. Stuart's Marine detachment storms the enginehouse where Brown, his sons, and a small force have barricaded themselves.

free the slaves, a feeling that was bolstered by letters found on Brown indicating he knew Frederick Douglass and other well-known abolitionists. In response, one hundred Virginia slave owners offered large rewards for the capture of Douglass and other abolitionists. Douglass fled the country until the excitement died down.

In the South, Brown was considered the devil incarnate. His raid was the living embodiment of the South's deepest fear that someone was going to organize and arm the slaves and turn them against their masters in an orgy of blood and death. Even in the North, Brown was initially thought to be insane.

But as newspapers throughout the country reported on Brown's trial, which took place in Charles Town, Virginia, in late October, the Northern perspective changed. As the wounded Brown was carried into the courtroom on a cot each day, Northern sympathy for him increased. He became not a lunatic but a sincere yet misguided man who had tried to end an evil practice the best way he knew how.

By the end of his trial, Brown had been transformed from a fanatic into a martyr for the antislavery cause. When he was found guilty and sentenced to be hanged, the poet Ralph Waldo Emerson said that he would "make the gallows as glorious as the cross."[46] Others called him a saint.

Brown added to the growing sympathy for him and his cause by speaking eloquently and passionately at his trial. Upon hearing his sentence, Brown rose from his cot and addressed the court:

Now, if it is deemed necessary that I should forfeit my life for the furtherance of the ends of justice and mingle my blood further with the blood of my children and with the blood of millions in this slave country, whose rights are disregarded by wicked, cruel, and unjust enactments, I say let it be done.[47]

As Brown awaited his execution, rumors flew of imminent rescue attempts. The only incident that occurred, however, was the shooting of a lost cow that wandered too close to the nervous soldiers guarding Brown's cell. On December 2, 1859, John Brown was hanged. The final message that he left for his fellow Americans was a chilling prophecy of the calamitous war that was about to come: "I, John Brown, am now quite certain that the crimes of this guilty land will never be purged away but with Blood."[48]

Others agreed. In New England, poet Henry Wadsworth Longfellow cast his eye at the growing storm clouds on the American horizon and wrote, "They [those who hanged Brown] are sowing the wind to reap the whirlwind, which will come soon."[49]

Controversial in Death

Feelings about Brown after his death reflected the deep division between North and South. New York *Tribune* editor Horace Greeley praised the grandeur and nobility of Brown and his men, whereas Richmond newspapers warned that the Harpers Ferry incident had significantly advanced the cause of Southern secession more than any other event since the formation of the federal government.

The vast difference of opinion over Brown's actions provided a vivid illustration of the problems facing the country as the United States entered the crucial presidential election year of 1860. Many Northern Democrats and Southerners blamed the "Black Republican" Party for poisoning people's beliefs about the South and creating the perfect environment for Brown's raid. Stephen A. Douglas, the likely Democratic nominee for president, said that the Republicans and their antislavery doctrine caused the incident at Harpers Ferry. Republicans tried to disavow Brown's actions but were drowned out by fire-breathing, pro-secessionist orators such as Georgia senator Robert Toombs, who warned Southerners to arm themselves against the "war" that Republicans were waging against the region and its institutions.

The Know-Nothing Party

While slavery wreaked havoc on the major political parties, it also opened the door for third parties to participate in the electoral process. One of these was the American Party, also known as the Know-Nothing Party.

Beginning in the early 1850s, the Know-Nothings capitalized on growing fears that the large number of immigrants pouring into the United States would not only take away jobs from native-born Americans but also exert "foreign influence" on the political process. The party grew quickly, fueled primarily by its members' intense hatred of Catholics (whom they believed were influenced by the Pope); the Know-Nothings felt that Catholics should be banned from ever holding any political office, no matter how insignificant. Members used coded signs and signals to recognize each other and avoid revealing information to outsiders,

prompting Horace Greeley to dub them the "Know-Nothings."

In 1854, the Know-Nothings elected members of state legislatures in Delaware and Pennsylvania and almost the entire legislature—as well as the governor—in Massachusetts. The following year, the party won control of state legislatures in Rhode Island, New Hampshire, Connecticut, Maryland, and Kentucky, and it made respectable showings in numerous other states.

In 1856, the Know-Nothings nominated former president Millard Fillmore as their presidential candidate. But by then, unable to implement any of their anti-Catholic and antiforeign ideas, and wracked by dissension over the slavery issue, the Know-Nothings were in decline. Although Fillmore polled 21 percent of the vote, he gained only Maryland's eight electoral votes. By the 1860 presidential election, the Know-Nothings had vanished.

As 1860 progressed, tensions increased between the two areas. Throughout the South, Northerners were either told to leave or chased out of town by armed mobs. As an Atlanta newspaper said, anyone who did not regard slavery as a blessing was an enemy of the South. Others flocked to join military groups organized to repel the abolitionist and Black Republican brigades that were supposedly gathering to invade the South.

Alarmed that secession seemed to be gaining momentum, others denounced Brown and his methods in an attempt to hold the fraying fabric of the Union together. In one week, twenty thousand New York City merchants signed a document calling for a public meeting to reassure the South of their good intentions.

But the North also did its share of saber-rattling. Typical of such inflammatory talk were the remarks made by labor leader and journalist August Willich, who told a Cincinnati audience to "nerve their arms for the day of retribution, when Slavery and Democracy [the Democratic Party] would be crushed in a common grave."[50]

Amid this talk of war and secession, Abraham Lincoln spoke at Cooper Union in New York City on February 27, 1860. It was the first time he had spoken in New York, and he worked long and hard on his speech, determined to show the sophisticated eastern audience that he was a polished public speaker. He also knew that making a good impression would greatly help his chances of being the Republican presidential nominee.

In his speech, Lincoln decried those who said that the election of a Republican president that fall would destroy the Union and that it would be the fault of those who voted for the Republicans. That would be, Lincoln said, like a "highwayman [who] holds a pistol to my ear, and mutters through his teeth, 'Stand and deliver, or I shall kill you, and then you will be a murderer!'"[51]

As for slavery, Lincoln repeated the Republican Party line and his own belief that slavery should be left alone where it already existed but must not be allowed to spread into the territories. However, he also warned his audience that compromises on slavery would soon be impossible and that everyone was going to have to take a stand. There was not a middle ground, he said, between those who supported slavery and those who opposed it. Lincoln ended his speech with words that are still quoted today: "Let us have faith that right makes might, and in that faith, let us, to the end, dare to do our duty as we understand it."[52]

The speech was extremely well received. (One New York reporter wrote that "No man ever before made such an impression on his first appeal to a New York audience")[53]. And it significantly boosted Lincoln's chances as a Republican presidential candidate.

Lincoln's address at Cooper Union in New York City (pictured) was extremely well received and boosted his chances for the presidency.

Two months later, the Democratic Party proved Lincoln correct by breaking apart over its failure to compromise on slavery. In April 1860, the party met in Charleston, South Carolina, to nominate a presidential candidate, but the convention quickly became derailed over slavery. Southern delegates demanded that the federal government promise to protect slavery in all the territories. They also asked for veto power over the party's presidential nominee, who was expected to be Stephen A. Douglas. (Douglas's support for popular sovereignty was anathema to pro-slavery forces, who didn't want to leave the question open to discussion.) When the Northern delegates rejected this ultimatum, the Southerners walked out, splintering the party. The Democrats had been the dominant political party in the United States for more than fifty years, but ultimately they could not survive the ruinous effects of slavery, which destroyed them just as it had previously destroyed the Whigs and the Know-Nothings.

Both halves of the Democratic Party eventually reconvened in different cities and nominated different presidential candidates. The Northern-dominated portion met in Baltimore and nominated Douglas; the Southern delegates gathered in Richmond and selected as their candidate President James Buchanan's vice president John C. Breckinridge.

To confuse matters even further, another new party—the Constitutional Union Party—also formed. Its presidential candidate was former Whig congressman and U.S. senator John Bell, running on a vague pledge (the party refused to adopt a platform) "to recognize no political principle other than the Constitution of the Country, the Union of the States, and the Enforcement of the Laws."[54]

Flushed with Presidential Fever

With the Democrats hopelessly split, and Bell's candidacy further separating potential Democratic votes, the path to the presidency was open for the Republicans. Lincoln, after his triumphant Cooper Union address and a subsequent successful speechmaking tour of New England, had returned to Springfield flushed with presidential fever. ("No man knows, when that Presidential grub gets to gnawing at him, just how deep in it will get until he has tried it,"[55] he once said.)

But other Republicans were just as eager as Lincoln was to take advantage of the Democrats' disintegration. Several candidates vied for the Republican presidential nomination at the party's convention in Chicago. The favorite was William H. Seward, former New York governor.

One by one, however, the other candidates fell by the wayside, until the nomination was a contest between Seward and Lincoln. Many Republicans worried that Seward's radical antislavery reputation would alienate many moderate voters. His close association with corrupt elements in New York City also tainted his candidacy.

The Constitutional Union Party

The Constitutional Union Party was a curious hodgepodge of disaffected members of other political parties. Remnants of the Whigs and Know-Nothings, plus voters who were lukewarm on the slavery issue, joined together during the 1860 presidential campaign to form the Constitutional Union Party.

Composed primarily of aged politicians from another era, the party's position on the most important issue of the day—slavery—was to pretend that it didn't exist. Instead of adopting a platform at its May 1860 convention, the party simply produced a vague, two-hundred-word statement that pledged support of the U.S. Constitution, the Union of states, and enforcement of the country's laws. The party nominated John Bell, former senator from Tennessee, as its presidential candidate. Bell was an appropriate choice for a party of leftovers, since he had begun his political career as a Democrat before switching to the Whigs.

In the 1860 presidential election, Bell and the Constitutional Unionists were nonfactors in the North. In the South, Bell battled Democrat John Breckinridge for votes. When the votes were tallied, Bell received 12 percent of the national vote and thirty-nine electoral votes (Kentucky, Tennessee, and Virginia). Despite this strong showing, however, the Constitutional Unionists were merely a party of the moment and did not survive past the election.

John Bell was the first and only presidential candidate of the Constitutional Union Party.

Lincoln, on the other hand, was a moderate, middle-of-the-road candidate, who had previously said he would leave slavery alone where it already existed. He was also the "Rail-Splitter" and "Honest Abe," a common, virtuous man whose rags-to-riches story appealed to a broad spectrum of voters. On the convention's fourth ballot, Lincoln won the Republican nomination for president. Maine senator Hannibal

This Republican political banner shows Lincoln and his vice presidential candidate, Maine senator Hannibal Hamlin.

Hamlin, a former Democrat, was selected vice president.

A State of Chaos

Thus the United States embarked on the most critical election in its young history with its political system in an unprecedented state of chaos. With the country's major political party hopelessly fragmented, another whose appeal was strictly regional, and yet another that refused to take a stand on any issue, the electoral process was a mirror image of America: divided and confused.

Even the campaign reflected sectional differences: In the North it was Lincoln versus Douglas, while in the South Breckinridge battled Bell. Reflecting their sectional appeal, Republicans did not even field a ticket in ten Southern states.

In keeping with the custom of the times, Lincoln did not campaign for himself and remained at home in Springfield, where he would address those who visited him. However, others spoke on his behalf; an estimated fifty thousand pro-Republican speeches were delivered.

Breckinridge also maintained a low profile in the campaign. He was a reluctant candidate who was mortified that his name was associated with the so-called secession convention. Although he felt slavery was guaranteed by the Constitution, he condemned the growing feeling in the South that Lincoln's election guaranteed secession.

Some have suggested that Breckinridge accepted the nomination of the "secession" wing of the Democrats to show the obviously unelectable Douglas and Bell the futility of their own candidacies. According to the theory, once everyone realized that they were splitting the anti-Lincoln vote, the three would withdraw, allowing the Democrats to unite on a single candidate to stop Lincoln.

Douglas, however, had no intention of withdrawing. Once Breckinridge learned this, he knew that his own candidacy was doomed as well. However, he had given his word to the convention and felt it would be dishonorable to withdraw, no matter how long the odds. "I trust I have the courage to lead a forlorn hope,"[56] he said.

Like Lincoln, Breckinridge hardly spoke on his own behalf during the campaign. Not a fire-breathing secessionist like many of his followers, Breckinridge preferred silence to the endorsement of extremist views. When he was attacked for failing to expound on his beliefs, he answered, "To those who take advantage of the position of a silent man, to heap upon him execrations, I say, pour it on, I can endure."[57]

Douglas, realizing how desperate his situation was, boldly broke with tradition and campaigned for himself. For months the "Little Giant" traveled throughout the country telling audiences that he was the only true national candidate and the only one who could save the Union from destruction.

Although already feeling the effects of the illness that would kill him in a year, Douglas bravely ventured into the South, defending the Union to antagonistic crowds, telling them that he would "hang every man higher than Haman who would attempt . . . to break up the Union by resistance to its laws."[58]

In October, Republicans swept state elections in Pennsylvania, Ohio, and Indiana. Douglas knew that this meant he would not win those states and that Lincoln now would almost certainly be elected president.

John C. Breckinridge

One of the leading Democratic politicians of the era, John C. Breckinridge had a bright political career that was cut short by the Civil War.

Born in Kentucky in 1821, Breckinridge served in the Mexican War before being elected to Kentucky's legislature in 1849. Elected to Congress in 1851 as a Democrat, from a district that had long been controlled by the Whig Party, Breckinridge quickly gained a following as a rising young political star. While in Congress, he was a key figure in getting the controversial Kansas-Nebraska Act passed, and many considered him the "power behind the throne" in the administration of President Franklin Pierce. In 1856, after considering a run for the Democratic presidential nomination, he became the party's choice for vice president, and he was elected along with James Buchanan in November 1856.

In 1859 he became senator-elect from Kentucky. But the following year, he reluctantly accepted the presidential nomination from the so-called Southern Wing of the Democratic Party when it split over the slavery issue. Although he was the only candidate to win states from more than one section of the country, he lost the election to Abraham Lincoln.

Returning to the Senate, he remained pro-Union but anti-Lincoln. Finally, considered a danger, Breckinridge went over to the Confederacy, although there was evidence that he was still a Union supporter.

As a brigadier general for the South, Breckinridge fought valiantly in a losing cause, and he served as the Confederacy's secretary of war during the last year of the war. After the war ended he fled to Europe but was finally granted amnesty and returned to the United States in February 1869. He died in May 1875.

"We must try to save the Union," said Douglas to his private secretary. "I will go South."[59] This was the Little Giant's finest

Stephen Douglas—or "Little Giant"—rose above partisan politics and devoted himself to preserving the Union.

hour; rising above partisan politics, Douglas again warned Southerners that the North would never tolerate secession without a fight. Ignoring threats, dodging objects hurled at him while speaking to hostile crowds, and struggling with his own failing health, Douglas continued his support of the Union.

However, delivered in a region and a climate so volatile that armed men marched with banners that linked resistance to Lincoln with obedience to God,

Douglas's exhortations fell on deaf ears. The South was swept up in a wave of fear, anger, and hysteria surpassing even that which followed John Brown's raid. Stories of murder, rape, and destruction by slaves incited by mysterious strangers from the North filled Southern newspapers and fueled secessionist talk. As the election drew closer, and the likelihood of a Lincoln victory became more apparent, the chorus of those advocating the destruction of the Union reached a shrill crescendo.

Benjamin Hill, the governor of Georgia, proclaimed, "This government and Black Republicanism cannot live together," while John J. Crittenden of Kentucky said that the South "has come to the conclusion that in case Lincoln should be elected . . . she could not submit to the consequences, and therefore, to avoid her fate, will secede from the Union."[60]

With both a Republican victory and secession seemingly a foregone conclusion, alarmed moderates turned to the one person they thought could stop it: Abraham Lincoln. Requests poured into him at Springfield to say something to pacify the South. Lincoln's reply was simple: He had already stated his position on slavery numerous times.

"What is it I could say which would quiet alarm?" he said in October 1860. "Is it that no interference by the government, with slaves or slavery within the states, is intended? I have said this so often already, that a repetition of it is but mockery, bearing an appearance of weakness."[61]

In reality, Lincoln was walking a thin line. Although he was loath to make statements that would make him seem cowed by secessionist threats, he also didn't want to alienate Southerners while there was still a chance of preserving the Union. Many areas of the South did not rely on cotton, were uninterested in slavery, and despised the rich plantation owners. "All they [plantation owners] want is to get you to fight for their infernal Negroes," said one small Alabama farmer, "and after you do their fightin', you may kiss their hin' parts for all they care."[62] To try and keep people like these loyal to the Union, Lincoln relied on his previous statements, hoping they would not provide fresh ammunition for secessionists.

Lincoln Elected

On November 6, 1860, Abraham Lincoln was elected the sixteenth president of the United States. He had 1,866,452 popular votes, followed by Douglas (1,376,957), Breckinridge (849,781), and Bell (588,879). In electoral votes, Lincoln received 180, followed by Breckinridge (72), Bell (39), and Douglas (12).

An analysis of the votes revealed the deep divisions cleaving the United States. Lincoln won all of the Northern states, as well as California and Oregon, but not one state in the South. Bell won Tennessee, Kentucky, and Virginia. The remaining Southern states, as well as the border states of Maryland and Delaware, went to Breckinridge. Douglas won Missouri outright and split New Jersey's electoral votes with Lincoln.

The other three candidates combined had nearly 1 million more votes than Lincoln, who didn't receive even one popular vote in ten Southern states. Overall, Lincoln received just 40 percent of the popular vote; he was a minority president in the strictest sense.

News of Abraham Lincoln's election is greeted coldly in Charleston, South Carolina. Lincoln did not win a single Southern state.

Lincoln spent election night in the Springfield telegraph office, keeping track of the returns. When it became clear he had won, he walked home and simply told his wife he had been elected. If he had any concerns about what the badly split vote meant for the country and for the job ahead of him, he kept them to himself.

The implications of the election quickly became clear. Southern moderates who had hoped to preserve the Union by voting for either Bell or Douglas now found themselves with no alternative to a Lincoln presidency but secession. "With your defeat, the cause of the Union was lost,"[63] wrote a Mobile, Alabama, newspaper editor to Douglas.

Others were less reserved in their feelings. An Atlanta newspaper thundered that even if "the Potomac is crimsoned in human gore . . . the South will never submit to such humiliation and degradation as the inauguration of Abraham Lincoln."[64]

In Springfield, Lincoln began choosing his cabinet and preparing for the long journey to Washington, D.C. Each day he received letters from people hoping that he would be burned, hanged, tortured, or killed before he could take office. Fortunately, not all his mail was so hateful. One man suggested that he have his food tasted to avoid being poisoned, and a woman told him of her dream about how to avoid war. Another writer, trying to be helpful, advised him to resign at his inauguration and appoint Stephen Douglas as president.

One piece of advice, however, Lincoln did take: When eleven-year-old Grace Bedell wrote that he would look better with a beard, he began growing one. But even the beard could not hide the fact that, by the night of his election, Lincoln, at age fifty-one, was far from the robust physical specimen that had once ferried flatboats down the Mississippi. His weight had dipped to about 180 pounds, and his stooped posture and tall, thin frame made him appear consumptive. With his large nose and ears, scrawny neck, and frequently unkempt hair, Lincoln was in marked contrast to his predecessor, the white-haired, aristocratic-looking James Buchanan.

Secessionist Fever

Although secessionist fever burned across the South in the weeks after Lincoln's election, some in the region rejected disunion and hoped for compromise with the North. To try and sway these moderates, secessionists raised the specter of racial equality. According to them, abolition of slavery and Black Republican rule were the first steps in the eventual equality of black and white. Secessionist speakers painted lurid images to rally support for their cause. "If you are tame enough to submit [to Republican rule]," warned South Carolina clergyman James Furman, "abolition preachers will be at hand to consummate the marriage of your daughters to black husbands."[65]

As this type of rhetoric reached a crescendo across the South, Lincoln was again besieged by pleas to reach an agreement with the Southern states to halt the apparently imminent destruction of the Union. But the president-elect was unmoved; he would not betray those who had supported both him and his party in the election by brokering a deal with the South that circumvented those principles. "By no act or complicity of mine, shall the Republican party become a mere sucked egg, all shell and no principle in it,"[66] he said.

Lincoln's Influence

Although Lincoln had no actual power to combat secession until his inauguration, he could influence events in other ways. When Senator John J. Crittenden proposed a series of largely pro-slavery, pro-Southern amendments to the U.S. Constitution in December 1860, Lincoln's response to congressional Republicans was quick and firm: "Entertain no proposition for a compromise in regard to the extension of slavery," he wrote, adding that such a plan would put the country on a "high-road to a slave empire."[67]

Lincoln also turned a deaf ear to those who blamed the Black Republicans for the secession threat and those who urged the party to abandon or modify its position on slavery before it was too late:

We have just carried an election on principles fairly stated to the people. Now we are told in advance, the government shall be broken up, unless we surrender to those we have beaten. . . . If we surrender, it is the end of us.[68]

However, all talk about compromise soon became academic. Barely more than a month after Lincoln's election, on December 20, 1860, South Carolina seceded from the Union. Sitting on the platform of the convention that unanimously ratified the secession ordinance was Edmund Ruffin, a Virginia planter and ardent secessionist who called South Carolina's action the happiest occasion of his life. In his hand he held one of the pikes that John Brown had carried in his attack on Harpers Ferry to arm the slaves. The long-threatened disintegration of the Union had begun.

The year 1860 had begun with the country still reeling from the effects of John Brown's raid. It ended with one of Brown's weapons being hoisted in the air as a symbol of revolution, not of slaves, as Brown had intended, but of slave owners. All across America, everyone wondered what the new year would bring.

Chapter 4

Caught Between Both Sides

outh Carolina's decision to leave the Union meant that secession, after years of being threatened, had turned into reality. The fraying fabric of the Union, stretched paper-thin by slavery, had finally torn.

Before it was completely shredded, however, politicians, business leaders, newspaper editors, and others desperately sought a last-ditch compromise that would keep other states from following South Carolina's example. Many Southerners thought the state's action incomprehensible; South Carolina, it was said, was too small for a republic, and too large for an insane asylum.

But efforts at reconciliation were in vain; no compromise on earth could reverse the election of Abraham Lincoln and the Southern fears of a "Black Republican" administration. As a North Carolinian explained to a friend in Massachusetts, the South did not fear Lincoln the individual but "the funda-

mental idea that underlies the whole movement of his nomination and canvass, & his election. It is the declaration of unceasing war against slavery as an institution." [69]

The New York *Herald* even advised Lincoln to quit before his inauguration so that he could be replaced by someone more agreeable to both North and South:

> If he persists in his present position . . . he will totter into a dishonoured grave, driven there perhaps by the hands of an assassin, leaving behind him a memory more execrable [detestable] than that of [Benedict] Arnold. [70]

As unrealistic as its suggestion was, the *Herald* had put forth the only "compromise" that could have saved the Union. Nothing short of Lincoln's resignation—before taking office—could allay Southern fears that the policies of a Republican administration would inevitably lead to a

A cartoon published in a Northern newspaper depicts the Southern states blindly following South Carolina off the cliff of secession.

massive and bloody slave uprising. Stories such as the one in which Baltimore police raided a gathering of free blacks and found a bust of John Brown, along with banners praising him, sent shudders throughout Southerners. Many figured it was only a matter of time until the Republicans adopted Brown's methods. "Now that the black radical Republicans have the power," said a South Carolinian, "I suppose they will [John] Brown us all."[71]

In this emotionally charged atmosphere, compromise was futile. As Lincoln had so accurately pointed out at Cooper Union, no middle ground could exist between those who opposed and those who supported slavery. The result was the complete shattering of the fragile bonds that held the Union together. One by one the states of the Deep South seceded: Mississippi left on January 10, 1861, followed by Florida, Alabama, Georgia, Louisiana, and Texas.

On February 4, 1861, delegates from the seven seceded states met in Montgomery, Alabama, to organize the Confederate States of America. Five days later, former Mississippi senator Jefferson Davis was elected president of the new nation.

A Nation Like No Other

This was a nation like no other, a country founded on the principle that one race was the master of another. As Confederate vice president Alexander Stephens explained, the new government was based

upon the great truth that the negro is not equal to the white man, that slavery—subordination to the superior race—is his natural and normal condition. This our new government is the first in the history of the world based upon this great physical, philosophical and moral truth.[72]

Meanwhile, as a new nation was being born in Alabama, the president-elect of the disintegrating United States of America was busy in Springfield packing trunks with clothing and papers and scrawling "A. Lincoln, The White House, Washington, D.C." on their tags. Around the time that Jefferson Davis was introduced as president of the Confederacy, Lincoln began the long journey by rail from Springfield to Washington.

Paramount among Lincoln's many worries as he headed for the nation's capital was how to keep the Union from splintering any further. States in the Upper South, such as North Carolina, Virginia, and Tennessee, had rejected secession for the moment, primarily be-

cause slavery was less prominent there. Only 20 percent of white families in the Upper South owned slaves, compared with 37 percent in those states that now constituted the Confederacy.

But the Upper South's loyalty to the Union was tenuous. Typical of the bellicose attitude among Upper South states was that displayed by Tennessee, which passed a resolution warning that its citizens would "resist [any] invasion of the soil of the South at any hazard and to the last extremity."[73] Not even yet in power, the fledgling Lincoln administration knew it would have to be very careful in its reaction to the Confederacy, or risk driving the Upper South states out of the Union as well.

Thus the president-elect and his fellow Republicans were careful not to say or do anything that would antagonize the Upper South between the time of the Deep South states' secession and Lincoln's inauguration on March 4, 1861. Although two days after South Carolina had seceded Lincoln had again tried to reassure the South, saying that it "would be in no more danger in this respect [an attack on slavery] than it was in the days of Washington,"[74] in general the president avoided controversial subjects. During the nearly two-week trip to Washington from Springfield, he made numerous stops and speeches, but they were general, almost trivial talks that steered clear of the secession crisis.

"There is nothing going wrong . . . nobody is suffering anything . . . there is

Jefferson Davis

"The man and the hour have met." With those words, Jefferson Davis was introduced to a cheering crowd as the first president of the Confederate States of America on February 16, 1861, in Montgomery, Alabama. Little did anyone suspect that the tall, thin, iron-willed Davis would also be the last president of the rebel nation.

Born in Kentucky on June 3, 1808, Davis served the United States in many different capacities: as a soldier, a congressman, a senator from Mississippi, and a secretary of war in the cabinet of President Franklin Pierce. He was a leading supporter of states' rights and slavery, and he became known as the spokesman for the Southern point of view in the increasingly bitter ideological battle with the North. Nevertheless, he did not favor secession and resigned his Senate seat only when Mississippi left the Union.

Despite misgivings over secession, Davis became the Confederate president and tried to build a nation in wartime. Hampered by a lack of funds and limited manufacturing capability, Davis hoped that diplomatic recognition from England or France would help turn the tide in the South's favor, but it never came. Davis's determination, and the superb military abilities of men like Robert E. Lee and Stonewall Jackson, helped sustain the South until the superior manpower and materials advantage of the North won out. At war's end Davis was captured by Northern soldiers in Georgia and charged with treason, but the case was ultimately dropped. He died in 1889.

Jefferson Davis was the first—and last—president of the Confederate States of America.

no crisis excepting such a one as may be gotten up at any time by designing politicians,"[75] were typical of statements made by the president-elect, who had also miscalculated the extent of Southern anger and considered secession the work of a small group of rich planters. Lincoln's ap-

parent indifference to secession sparked alarm among many, who thought him of inferior character.

Although in public Lincoln projected an image of calm in the face of the storm of disunion, privately he chafed at the four-month delay between his election and the inauguration. Momentous events were happening, and even though he was the president-elect, he was powerless to do anything until he took office. "I only wish I could have got to Washington to lock the door before the horse was stolen," he said after the Deep South states had seceded. "But when I get to the spot I can find only the tracks."[76]

In his inaugural address in Washington, D.C. (pictured), Lincoln (center) assured the South that he would not abolish slavery in the states in which it existed.

Lincoln Takes Office

Finally, on March 4, Lincoln was sworn in as the sixteenth president of the United States. In his inaugural address, Lincoln painted a picture of hope and moderation in an appeal to the Confederacy:

My countrymen, one and all, think calmly and well, upon this whole subject. Nothing valuable can be lost by taking time. In your hands, my dissatisfied fellow countrymen, and not in mine, is the momentous issue of civil war. The government will not assail you. You can have no conflict without being yourselves the aggressors.[77]

In the same speech, he again reassured the South, particularly those states that had not yet seceded, that it had nothing to fear from his administration concerning slavery: "I have no purpose, directly or indirectly, to interfere with the institution of slavery in the States where it exists. I believe

I have no lawful right to do so, and I have no inclination to do so."[78]

If Lincoln hoped that this speech would buy him time to seek a peaceful solution to the secession crisis, he quickly discovered that time was the one thing he did not have. The day after his inauguration, he learned that Fort Sumter in South Carolina's Charleston Harbor, one of the few Union forts in Confederate territory that had not been seized by the rebel government, was running out of supplies. Virtually surrounded by Southern troops, the fort could not hold without supplies being sent by the federal government.

Only one day into his term as president, Lincoln was faced with a critical decision: If he sent the supplies by ships that would have to fight their way into the harbor, he would be the one who started a war. If he withdrew the garrison and surrendered the fort, not only would he seem like a weak leader, but he risked destroying the embryonic Republican Party, discouraging the Northern states, and, perhaps, shattering the Union forever.

Lincoln decided to resupply the fort peacefully, without firing at the Confederates, and sent a message to them explaining his intentions. Meanwhile, pro-secessionists in the Upper South urged that Fort Sumter be attacked, in order to draw those states into the Confederacy. "The shedding of blood," said Edmund Ruffin, "will serve to change many voters in the hesitating states, from the submission or procrastinating ranks, to the zealous for immediate secession." [79]

Roger Pryor, another Virginian who favored secession, put it more simply to the people in Charleston: "If you want us to join you, strike a blow!" [80]

With Lincoln's supply ships steaming toward Fort Sumter, Jefferson Davis and the Confederate government made the fateful decision to attack the fort before they could arrive. At 4:30 A.M. on April 12, 1861, the Confederate cannons surrounding Fort Sumter opened fire; according to legend, Edmund Ruffin helped fire the first shot. The civil war that all had dreaded but no one knew how to stop had begun.

After a thirty-three-hour bombardment, Fort Sumter fell on April 14. The next day, Lincoln called for seventy-five thousand militiamen to serve for ninety days to subdue the rebellion. In response, four Upper South states seceded: Virginia, Arkansas, Tennessee, and North Carolina. Kentucky, Maryland, and Missouri did not leave the Union, but, because of their large pro-secessionist

Edmund Ruffin (top), Fort Sumter (below).

populations, there existed a threat that they might join the Confederacy at any time.

Now that war had come, it was a time for choosing sides. Stephen A. Douglas said that a man must be for the United States or against it. One month later, the Little Giant was dead.

Lincoln Loses Robert E. Lee

One man who did reluctantly choose sides was Robert E. Lee. Although loyal to the Union, he was more devoted to his home state of Virginia. When Virginia seceded, Lee resigned from the U.S. army, and the North lost the man whom Lincoln had wanted to put in charge of the Union armies.

If Southern slaveholders were pleased that war had finally come, so too were some abolitionists. To them, war meant that a critical juncture had been reached in the struggle against slavery and that the battle would now be fought with bullets instead of words. Many agreed with Frederick Douglass that the slaveholders themselves had immensely helped the antislavery cause by their recklessness in agitating for war. While many in the North may have let the slave states secede untouched, the outbreak of hostilities hardened attitudes toward the Confederacy and its institutions, including slavery.

"A few weeks ago I would have consented to let the slave states go without requiring the abolition of slavery," said abolitionist Gerrit Smith. "But now, since the Southern tiger has smeared himself with our blood, we will not, if we get him in our power, let him go without having drawn his teeth and claws."[81]

Ironically, although slavery was a primary cause of the war, both sides initially tried to ignore it and portray the war as being fought for other reasons.

Once the war began, the Confederacy found slavery—one of its bedrock principles—to be a millstone around its neck. As Southerners reached out to other countries, both to establish the legitimacy of their government and to seek alliances, they found slavery was blocking their efforts. No country wanted to recognize a government that legitimized the barbaric practice of slavery. In May 1861, Southern commissioners to Great Britain wrote that

The public mind here is entirely opposed to the Government of the Confederate States of America on the question of slavery. . . . The sincerity and universality of this feeling embarrass the Government in dealing with the question of our recognition.[82]

Realizing that slavery was making it a pariah among nations, the South claimed that it was fighting to gain its liberty and right of self-government from the North, rather than because of slavery.

In the North, the antislavery Republican Party also tried to downplay the significance of slavery as a reason for the war. Lincoln knew that many Northerners were not abolitionists (Northern soldiers sang pro-Union, antiblack songs as they marched), so he presented the war as a fight to preserve the Union. Typical of the Northern view was that of newspaper editor Parson Brownlow, who said that, although he was against abolition, he was for the Union and so would fight the South "till Hell froze over and then fight on the ice."[83]

Others in the North, however, urged Lincoln to turn the war into a crusade to destroy slavery once and for all. "Any attempt to separate the freedom of the slave from the victory of the Government," said Frederick Douglass in May 1861,

any attempt to secure peace to the whites while leaving the blacks in chains . . . will be labor lost. The American people and the Government at Washington may refuse to recognize it for a time; but the "inexorable logic of events" will force it upon them in the end; that the war now being waged in this land is a war for and against slavery; and that it can never be effectually put down till one or the other of these vital forces is completely destroyed.[84]

Another influential Northern voice, former slave Harriet Tubman, also advocated using the war as a tool to destroy slavery. "God won't let Master Lincoln beat the South until he does the right thing," she wrote. "Master Lincoln, he's a great man and I'm a poor Negro but this Negro can tell Master Lincoln how to save money and young men. He can do it by setting the Negroes free."[85]

Some members of Lincoln's own party went even farther, urging him to destroy not just slavery but the Southern way of life that nurtured it. "We must treat this [war] as a radical revolution," said Republican Thaddeus Stevens, "and free every slave—slay every traitor—burn every rebel mansion, if these things be necessary [to preserve the country.]"[86]

Caught in the Middle

Lincoln was caught between both sides. As much as he personally wanted to eliminate slavery, he wanted even more to keep the three border states—Kentucky, Missouri, and Maryland—from joining the Confederacy. Lincoln viewed Kentucky, the state of his birth, as the linchpin that held the rest of the border states out of the Confederacy.

"I think to lose Kentucky is nearly the same as to lose the whole game," Lincoln wrote. "Kentucky gone, we can not hold Missouri, nor, as I think, Maryland. These all against us, and the job on our hands is too large for us."[87] Another time, the president commented that, while he would like to have God on his side in the war, he *must* have Kentucky.

Another reason that Lincoln ignored slavery at the beginning of the war was the need to keep the remaining Union states

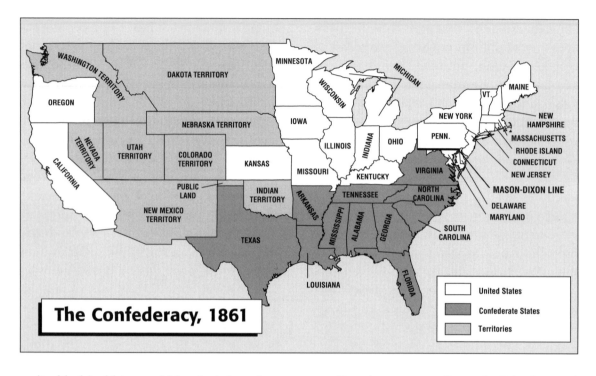

The Confederacy, 1861

Legend:
- United States
- Confederate States
- Territories

united behind him and his administration. In the election, he had won less than half the popular votes in the Union and border states; those who had not voted for him, and even some of those who had, might not support a war intended to destroy slavery. By making the war a means to preserve the Union, Lincoln was appealing to the patriotic instincts of *all* Northerners—pro- and antislavery.

Even some abolitionists, as anxious as they were to see slavery crushed, realized that it was wiser not to press their demands too soon. William Lloyd Garrison preached patience to his fellow abolitionists. But Wendell Phillips attacked the president for not even hinting that the purpose of the war was to end slavery.

Despite pressure from abolitionists and antislavery Republicans, Lincoln stuck to his policy of fighting the war because secession was illegal. On July 4, 1861, before a special session of Congress, Lincoln reiterated these views, repeating yet again that he had "no purpose, directly or indirectly, to interfere with slavery in the States where it exists."[88]

The Congress agreed with the president's policy. Later in July, the House and Senate passed similar resolutions stating that the war was not intended to overthrow or interfere with the rights or established institutions of the seceded states (i.e., slavery). According to the resolution, the conflict's purpose was "to defend and maintain the supremacy of the

Constitution and to preserve the Union with all the dignity, equality, and rights of the several States unimpaired."[89]

But slavery would not be ignored. The slaves themselves quickly realized that a war being fought by two powers on opposite sides of the slavery issue *had* to be about slavery at its core. They decided to take matters into their own hands. A few weeks after the fall of Fort Sumter, three slaves who had been working on Southern fortifications escaped to Union-held Fortress Monroe, Virginia, which was commanded by General Benjamin Butler.

The next day, a Confederate colonel who owned the slaves appeared at Fortress Monroe under a flag of truce and demanded the return of his "property," according to the Fugitive Slave Law. Butler, however, refused, pointing out that the Fugitive Slave Law did not affect a foreign

country, which Virginia claimed to be. Calling the slaves "contraband of war," Butler kept them and put them to work building a bakehouse for his own soldiers.

When the Lincoln administration approved Butler's decision, the tiny trickle that had begun with three slaves turned into a flood. By July 1861, approximately one thousand "contrabands" were at Fortress Monroe, forcing the Union government to define their legal status.

On August 6, Congress addressed the matter in a circular fashion by passing a confiscation act. Under this law, the contrabands were no longer slaves only if they had been working directly for the Confederate armed forces. However, the

Led by a Union officer, "contraband" blacks begin their workday at Fortress Monroe. By July 1861, approximately one thousand were at the fort.

law was silent about whether or not the contrabands were then free if they ceased to be slaves.

Although abolitionists were disappointed that the law did not go farther, even this halfhearted slap at slavery turned congressional Democrats and border-state legislators against the Lincoln administration. All but three voted against the bill, sending Lincoln a clear signal that his go-slow policy on slavery was the only way to avoid a split in Northern support for the war.

Fremont Blunders

But even the president could not control everything. In late July 1861, Lincoln sent John C. Fremont, the Republican Party's 1856 presidential candidate, to Missouri to head military operations against the Confederacy in the West. Fremont, however, turned out to be a bad general, and an even worse politician. After being beaten in battle by the rebels, Fremont compounded his woes by issuing a grandiose proclamation on August 30 that, in part, freed the slaves of all Confederate activists in Missouri.

Once again slavery was at the forefront of the war, exactly where Lincoln did not want it. Warning Fremont that freeing the slaves would alarm Southerners loyal to the Union, as well as possibly push Kentucky into the Confederacy, Lincoln asked him to modify his proclamation. In response, Fremont sent his wife, Jessie, to Washington to plead his case. When Lincoln met Mrs. Fremont, he told

her: "[This is] a war for a great national idea, the Union, and General Fremont should not have dragged the negro into it."[90] After getting nowhere with either Fremont or his wife, Lincoln ordered the general to modify his proclamation.

The Fremont controversy again put Lincoln between pro- and antislavery forces. Abolitionists and radical Republicans were outraged that Lincoln ordered the proclamation rescinded. The Cincinnati *Gazette* reported that people ripped portraits of Lincoln off their walls and trampled them underfoot in anger. Fremont, on the other hand, was showered with praise by abolitionist Henry Ward Beecher. Others, however, such as the New York *Herald*, praised the president for gently but firmly rebuking Fremont's actions.

Even Lincoln's friends were divided over his decision. William Herndon said that "Fremont's proclamation was right. Lincoln's modification of it was wrong."[91] In Kentucky, however, Joshua Speed had urged the president not to "allow us by the foolish action of a military popinjay to be driven from our present active loyalty."[92]

Complicating the Fremont situation was the status of the war. The Union army's defeat by the Confederates at Bull Run in July 1861 made it plain that the war was not going to be the brief, three-month affair Northerners thought but, rather, a long and bitter struggle. Conversely, Lincoln's call for 1 million troops to serve a three-year hitch after Bull Run demonstrated to the South the extent of Northern determination to continue fighting.

As each side dug in for a protracted conflict, they sought ways to hurt their opponent's ability to wage war. One thing that occurred to many Northerners was that slavery gave the South a huge advantage. Every slave that worked in the fields, built fortifications, or toiled in a factory freed another Southerner to fight. Slaves constituted more than 50 percent of the Confederacy's labor force; Union loyalists thought it foolish not to strike at so vital a component of the Southern war machine.

"To fight against slave-holders, without fighting against slavery, is but a half-hearted business, and paralyzes the hands engaged in it," said Frederick Douglass. "Fire must be met with water . . . war for the destruction of liberty must be met with war for the destruction of slavery."[93]

The president's policy of going slow on slavery to appease the border states was also losing support. "It is said we must consult the border states," said a Republican from Connecticut. "Permit me to say damn the border states."[94]

Even those who should have been Lincoln's natural allies, antislavery groups, were growing impatient with him. The American Anti-Slavery Society described Lincoln as "under the delusion that soft words will salve the nation's sore."[95]

Without a firm administration policy on slavery, Union military commanders were left to their own devices about how to treat runaway slaves, and they came up

The First Battle of Bull Run

It was the first battle of Bull Run (or Manassas) that convinced both North and South that what many thought would be a quick war might instead turn out to be something far more lengthy and bloody.

The battle was fought on July 21, 1861, between Union troops under General Irvin McDowell and Confederate soldiers commanded by General Pierre Gustave Toutant Beauregard. Goaded by the hysterical headlines of the *New York Tribune* that cried "On to Richmond!" and prodded by President Lincoln (who had called for troops for only ninety days and was anxious to see them used), the still-green Union army marched into Virginia. There, at a small stream called Bull Run, they encountered the also-untested rebel army. As the battle began, many civilians from Washington, D.C., who had followed the federal army, unfolded picnic lunches, opened bottles of wine, and settled down to enjoy the show.

Initially the battle went well for the Union, as they forced the Confederates to retreat. But, rallying around troops commanded by General Thomas J. Jackson, who stood as firm as a "stone wall," the Confederates counterattacked and drove the disorganized Northerners from the field. Soldiers and civilians alike streamed back to Washington, the images of killed and wounded men horribly etched in their minds. Nobody thought it was going to be a ninety-day war anymore.

with a variety of methods. General Henry Halleck refused to allow runaways to enter his camp; General William T. Sherman permitted it but also allowed their masters to look for them if they swore a loyalty oath to the Union. One Massachusetts colonel came up with perhaps the most unique solution: He put both the runaway slave and his master out of his camp at the same time. If the slave could outrun his master, he was free.

Not Ready for Slaves with Guns

As the war continued into the later months of 1861, calls for arming slaves grew, and so did the pressure on Lincoln's slavery policy. Thaddeus Stevens told the president that giving guns to slaves would be a formidable weapon for the Union. Wearily, Lincoln replied that the country was not yet ready for the sight of slaves with guns. Be patient, he advised, and possibly that day would come.

December brought more slavery trouble for the beleaguered president. On December 1, without first consulting with Lincoln, Secretary of War Simon Cameron released his annual report to the public. In one potentially explosive paragraph, Cameron wrote,

> It is as clearly a right of the Government to arm slaves, when it becomes necessary, as it is to use gun-powder taken from the enemy. If it shall be found that the men who have been held by the rebels are capable of bearing arms and performing efficient military service, it is the right, and may become the duty of the Government to arm and equip them, and employ their services against the rebels.[96]

Although Lincoln tried to recall the report and have Cameron delete this section, some newspapers printed it.

But the growing realization in the country that the war was going to be longer and bloodier than anticipated was causing a change in mood toward the South and toward slavery. Congress demonstrated this newfound resolve in late December, when the House of Representatives refused to reaffirm the resolution it had passed just a few months earlier that rejected slavery as a cause for the war. Instead, not only did Republican congressmen attack slavery, but antislavery bills began to be introduced.

Still wary of how total slave emancipation would affect the border states, Lincoln nevertheless also sensed that the tide of popular opinion was turning against slavery. On March 6, 1862, he urged Congress to pass a resolution offering financial aid to any state that adopted a system to gradually abolish slavery. Unsure of how such a proposal might be greeted, he presented it as a means of shortening the war, saying that if the border states freed their slaves the Confederacy would realize that they would never join it, and their will to fight would diminish.

Although Congress passed this resolution in April, the legislative pendulum was rapidly swinging toward even harsher measures. On March 13, 1862, Congress passed a new article of war forbidding army officers to return fugitive slaves to their masters. This finally resolved how

Dead soldiers litter a field after a battle. Such losses prompted the Union and the Confederacy to realize that they were in a fight to the death.

during his term in Congress, Lincoln himself had advocated this measure, and now it had finally happened. Not only did Congress provide federal funds to pay the slave owners, but it also promised steamship tickets to Liberia or Haiti to any freed slave. Lincoln favored colonization as part of emancipation, and he was pleased that Congress agreed with him.

But Congress was not yet done attacking slavery. In June, it banned slavery in the territories, thus finally settling the issue that had so much to do with causing the war. In July 1862 came two more laws: The first authorized the president to enroll blacks for "any war service for which they may be found competent,"[97] including military service. The second measure declared that the slaves of owners who supported the South were "forever free."

Slave Losses Mount

As the news of these new laws filtered southward, reaction was immediate. In North Carolina, $1 million worth of slaves disappeared in a single week. Georgians estimated that their losses in runaway slaves could reach $15 million. South Carolinians began moving their slaves to Texas, to make it more difficult for them to escape to Union lines.

Union commanders were to treat runaway slaves.

This, however, was just the beginning. One year earlier, before Bull Run, when everyone thought the war would be brief, it would have been inconceivable for Congress to move so forcefully against slavery, but a lifetime of battles fought and lives lost had passed since then. The mood of the country, and its lawmakers, reflected the growing feeling that they were in a fight to the death.

In April 1862 Congress abolished slavery in the District of Columbia. Long ago,

Frederick Douglass

Perhaps the single most influential voice arguing for freedom from slavery was this former slave who rose to become a role model for a nation.

He was born on February 7, 1817, in Maryland as Frederick Augustus Washington Bailey, the son of a slave. In 1838 he escaped to New Bedford, Massachusetts, and took the last name *Douglass*. In 1841, he spontaneously addressed an antislavery convention in Nantucket, Massachusetts, and his oratory was so powerful that he was hired as a speaker for the Massachusetts Anti-Slavery Society.

Douglass spoke against the evils of slavery both in America and abroad, helping to convert thousands to the abolitionist cause. He campaigned for Abraham Lincoln during the election of 1860. Once the Civil War began, Douglass continually pressed Lincoln and the North to use black troops in the struggle. Two of Douglass's sons were in the all-black 54th Massachusetts Regiment.

After the war, Douglass served in a variety of governmental posts, including as minister to Haiti from 1889 to 1891. He died on February 20, 1895.

Frederick Douglass

So many antislavery measures were pouring out of Washington that Frederick Douglass said it felt like a dream, but something even more profound was about to occur. On July 12, 1862, Lincoln summoned border-state congressmen to the White House and again urged that they support his plan for compensated, gradual emancipation. Warning that events were inexorably moving against slavery, the president said that if they didn't voluntarily decide to free their slaves, the institution itself would be extinguished anyway, "and you will have nothing valuable in lieu of it."[98]

But again, Lincoln's words fell on deaf ears. Instead of embracing the president's proposal, many border-state congressmen signed a manifesto rejecting it, citing the cost, the radical change it would cause in social structure, and the belief that slavery should be handled by the states, not the federal government.

But what these congressmen did not know was that, in rejecting this appeal, they had finally exhausted Lincoln's patience. Tired of trying to persuade them of the logic of his arguments, and realizing that the reason for the war had to be altered, the president had decided to adopt a new and much more radical approach to the slavery problem. The day he received the border-state manifesto, Lincoln told two of his cabinet members of his intention to issue a very special document on slavery—an emancipation proclamation.

Chapter 5

The Emancipation Proclamation

For a public servant like Abraham Lincoln, being elected president of the United States was the ultimate achievement. Unfortunately, because of the trials and tribulations he endured as chief executive, both in his personal and public life, he derived little joy from reaching the highest office in the land. Hounded by office-seekers, haunted by staggering casualty lists, besieged by problems stemming from the war, reviled and ridiculed by his opponents, Lincoln frequently felt isolated and trapped in the White House. "I am the loneliest man in America,"[99] he said after news of yet another Union military defeat.

As Lincoln searched desperately for a general who could match the Confederacy's wily Robert E. Lee, the Union armies were frequently beaten, and beaten badly. These losses affected the president deeply; after learning of the terrible slaughter of Union troops at the Battle of Fredericksburg, the president

wrung his hands and moaned, "What has God put me in this place for?" When a similar carnage of Northern soldiers occurred at the Battle of Chancellorsville,

The search for a Union general who could match Robert E. Lee (pictured) was a desperate one for Abraham Lincoln.

the distraught Lincoln cried, "My God! This is more than I can endure!"[100] He was so inconsolable over the loss of life that Secretary of War Edwin Stanton (who had replaced Simon Cameron) feared he might commit suicide.

Lincoln Succumbs to Despair

Although he had great strength of character and his determination to carry out the war to its conclusion helped steer the Union through its darkest hours, Lincoln sometimes succumbed to despair. Once, after yet more bad military news, Lincoln said sadly, "If hell is [not] any worse than this, it has no terror for me."[101]

The president sometimes tried to escape the pressure by playing with his children and their friends. Once, when the youngsters were debating whether to execute a soldier doll named Jack for sleeping while on guard duty, the president stopped working, listened to the pros and cons of the case against Jack very carefully, and then solemnly wrote on a piece of White House stationery: "The doll Jack is pardoned. By order of the President. A Lincoln."[102]

But even here, tragedy stalked Lincoln. On February 20, 1862, eleven-year-old Willie Lincoln, the son most like his father, died of typhoid fever in the White House. "It is hard, hard, hard to have him die!"[103] cried the heartbroken presi-

dent as he looked at Willie's body. Mary Lincoln lost herself in grief over her son's death, her moods swinging wildly from loud crying to silent despair for months. But Lincoln was barely afforded the luxury of grieving because of the many pressing problems that demanded his attention.

One of these problems was, of course, slavery. Hardly a day went by without either a pro-slavery or an antislavery representative lecturing him on his particular point of view. Once, after listening to yet another group harangue him, the harried president told a story about a man in debt who was constantly hounded by his creditor to pay the money he owed. Finally, at his wit's end, all the man could think to do was act crazy whenever he was asked for the money.

The death of Lincoln's son Willie (second from left) was a devastating blow to the president, who barely had time to grieve.

"I have on more than one occasion in this room, when beset by extremists on this question [slavery], been compelled to appear very mad," concluded Lincoln. "I think none of you will ever dispose of this subject without getting mad."[104]

Ever since he had been elected president, the slavery issue had hung over Lincoln like a sword of Damocles, threatening to destroy the infant Republican Party, the Union, and even the president himself. Realizing the possible disruptive effect that any sudden change in slave status would have on the social and economic structure of both North and South, Lincoln initially advocated gradual emancipation, with slave owners being paid for their losses and slaves given the choice of beginning life anew in another country.

That policy, however, earned Lincoln the scorn of both anti- and pro-slavery groups. While abolitionists like William Lloyd Garrison accused Lincoln of being soft on slavery, Archbishop John Hughes warned that most Union troops had not the slightest intention of fighting a war to satisfy a handful of abolitionists.

The Democratic Party also kept the racial pot boiling by playing to one of its natural constituencies, lower-class laborers. Democratic charges that the Black Republicans planned to free "two or three million semi-savages" to "overrun the North and enter into competition with the white laboring masses"[105] sometimes caused violence. In Cincinnati, black neighborhoods were attacked when striking Irish dockworkers were replaced by blacks; in Illinois, farmers rioted when the War Department tried to use "contrabands" to gather crops.

The Emancipation Proclamation

But even as extremists on both sides berated the president, Lincoln's position on slavery was shifting. On July 13, 1862, the day that border-state politicians rejected his latest plea to embrace compensated, gradual emancipation, Lincoln told Secretary of State William Seward and Secretary of the Navy Gideon Welles that, after thinking about it for weeks, he had decided to issue an emancipation proclamation that would unilaterally end slavery. Lincoln summed up his reasoning in one concise sentence that yet spoke volumes: "We must free the slaves or be ourselves subdued."[106]

On July 22, Lincoln told his entire cabinet about the Emancipation Proclamation. Their overall reaction was favorable; only Postmaster General Montgomery Blair expressed doubt, fearing that it would hurt the Republicans in the upcoming autumn election by opening them up to charges of being abolitionists.

The most logical suggestion came from Seward, who recommended not issuing the proclamation until it was supported by military success. Otherwise, he said, it would smack of desperation and be seen as "the last measure of an exhausted government, a cry for help, our last shriek, on the retreat."[107] Lincoln

William H. Seward

Although he was once a political rival of Abraham Lincoln, William H. Seward eventually became the president's friend and one of his most trusted advisers.

Born in New York in 1801, Seward quickly rose through the ranks to become the state's governor from 1839 to 1843. He also served as a U.S. senator from New York from 1849 to 1861. During this time he became a staunch abolitionist. He was a leading figure in the formation of the Republican Party and was considered the front-runner for the party's presidential nomination in 1860. However, his rigid antislavery credentials hurt him, and enabled Lincoln to wrest the nomination from him.

When he became Lincoln's secretary of state, Seward assumed that he would be almost a "shadow" president, directing foreign policy on his own initiative and, in general, setting the tone for the administration. However, after being told politely but firmly by Lincoln that he was the only one in charge, Seward realized he had underestimated the president. Thereafter Seward became one of Lincoln's most reliable advisers.

When Lincoln was assassinated, Seward was attacked and seriously wounded by another of the conspirators, but he survived and remained secretary of state under Andrew Johnson. In 1867 he purchased Alaska from Russia for $7.2 million; the deal was called "Seward's Folly" because Alaska was considered worthless, frozen ground. Seward died in 1872.

William Henry Seward served as Lincoln's secretary of state.

thought this was good advice, so he put the proclamation aside and waited for the Union forces to win a victory.

There were several reasons why Lincoln changed his mind about freeing the slaves all at once via an emancipation proclamation. Certainly, his lifelong belief that slavery was wrong and that he could wipe it away with the stroke of his pen was a factor. (He once said that whenever he heard anyone arguing for slavery, he felt a strong impulse to see that person treated as a slave.) Another factor was Lincoln's sense that the North must change its strategy or it would lose the war; this meant denying the Confederacy the use of slave labor to keep farms and factories functioning while white men went off to fight.

Another important reason for the timing of the proclamation was that Lincoln hoped it would stop European countries from formally recognizing the Confederacy. Formal diplomatic recognition by one of the European powers such as England or France had been sought by the Confederacy since its formation. It not only would bring the Southern government legitimacy in the eyes of the world, but it might also lead to other nation's accepting the notion that the Union was forever split. If that happened, and the Confederacy began receiving aid from Europe, Lincoln knew that the North's chances of defeating the South would be severely handicapped.

A Formidable Weapon

In the summer of 1862, Lincoln received word from Union diplomats in Europe that recognition of the Confederacy was near. One way to stop it was for the North to turn the war into a crusade to free the slaves; no European country wanted to grant diplomatic recognition to a nation that advocated slavery. Thus an emancipation proclamation was a formidable weapon that would enable Lincoln to turn one of the pillars of the Southern nation against itself.

However, this weapon would remain idle until the Union army won a victory. As he waited, the president continued to be criticized by antislavery advocates who charged that he was dragging his feet on emancipation. Perhaps the most cutting of these remarks came from Horace Greeley, who on August 19, 1862, published in the *Tribune* an emancipation plea entitled "The Prayer of Twenty Millions." In it, Greeley charged the president with being "disastrously remiss in the discharge of your official and imperative duty" concerning emancipation and said that Lincoln was "unduly influenced by the counsels, the representations, the menace of certain fossil politicians hailing from the border slave States."[108]

Horace Greeley (pictured) charged that Lincoln was not doing all he could in the pursuit of freedom for the slaves.

"On the face of this wide earth, Mr. President," continued Greeley, "there is not one disinterested, determined, intelligent champion of the Union cause who does not feel that all attempts to put down the Rebellion and at the same time uphold its inciting cause are preposterous and futile."[109]

In a masterfully written reply, Lincoln explained his views on the war and slavery to both Greeley and the country:

> My paramount object in this struggle is to save the Union, and is not either to save or to destroy slavery. If I could save the Union without freeing any slave, I would do it, and if I could save it by freeing all the slaves I would do it; and if I could save it by freeing some and leaving others alone I would also do that. What I do about slavery, and the colored race, I do because I believe it helps to save the Union.[110]

Lincoln Advocates Colonization

Meanwhile, even as the Emancipation Proclamation sat on his desk, Lincoln continued to advocate colonization of freed slaves. Before an audience of free black leaders at the White House in mid-August 1862, Lincoln again urged establishing a colony in Central America to which emancipated blacks could emigrate. The president said that, even once they were free, blacks would face a difficult time achieving equality in the United States: "There is an unwillingness on the part of our people,

harsh as it may be, for you free colored people to remain among us."[111]

The black leaders listened politely but coolly to the president's proposal. "This is our country as much as it is yours," said one man, "and we will not leave it."[112] The black newspaper *Anglo-African* called for the colonization of reluctant slave owners instead.

Ultimately, Lincoln persuaded Congress to appropriate $600,000 for colonization. In 1863, a group of 453 government-sponsored colonists were settled on an island near Haiti. One year later 368 survivors returned, beaten by starvation and smallpox. No more colonization efforts were attempted.

As Lincoln patiently waited for a military victory to justify issuing the Emancipation Proclamation, he tried to increase feelings against slavery in the country to soften the blow of the proclamation when it became public knowledge.

"We shall need all the antislavery feeling in the country, and more," Lincoln told a pair of antislavery clergymen at the White House, without revealing his future plans. "You can go home and try to bring the people to your views; and you may say anything you like about me, if that will help. Don't spare me!"[113]

During this time, Lincoln gave no indication that he had changed his position on slavery. Speaking before an antislavery group on September 13, the president agreed that slavery was the primary cause of the war, but he also noted that, at present, he couldn't even enforce the Constitution in the seceded states. Given those circumstances, he asked, "What good would a proclamation of emancipation from me do? I do not want to issue a document that the whole world will necessarily see must be inoperative."[114]

Four days later, on September 17, the president's long wait for a military victory finally ended. At the Maryland village of Sharpsburg, along the Antietam Creek, Union forces under General George McClellan turned back an invasion of the North by the Confederate Army of

Battle of Antietam

Antietam (or Sharpsburg) ranks among the most important battles of the Civil War. Although the battle itself was virtually a stalemate, it stopped the Confederate invasion of the North and gave Lincoln the victory he needed to announce his Emancipation Proclamation.

In September 1862 Southern forces invaded the North, driving into Maryland. Moving to meet them, Union troops found a copy of Confederate general Robert E. Lee's secret orders wrapped around three cigars. McClellan learned that Lee had divided his army into four parts. If he moved quickly, McClellan, with overwhelming superiority in numbers, could crush all four parts, virtually ending the war.

As usual, however, McClellan moved too slowly, allowing Lee time to gather his forces. The two sides ultimately clashed on September 17, 1862, near the town of Sharpsburg, Maryland, by the Antietam Creek. The battle turned on McClellan's failure to exploit several gaping holes in the Confederate lines; if he would have sent in his reserves to exploit these advantages, he might have destroyed Lee's army. But McClellan's customary caution won out and he did nothing, allowing the South to gather its battered forces and retreat the following day, to fight on for almost three more years. The Battle of Antietam was the single bloodiest day of the war.

Although hardly the decisive victory that he had hoped for, Lincoln used Antietam to issue his preliminary Emancipation Proclamation. For the time being, the South's retreat also ended speculation that Great Britain and France were about to formally recognize the Confederacy.

The marginal Union victory at Antietam prompted Lincoln to issue his preliminary Emancipation Proclamation.

Northern Virginia under Robert E. Lee. Poor decisions on the part of Union commanders prevented the Battle of Antietam from being the momentous victory it could have been, but it was enough to set the wheels in motion to issue the Emancipation Proclamation.

(Ironically, the victory that set the stage for emancipation was won by a Union general with pro-slavery leanings. Early in July, when Lincoln visited the Union army camp, McClellan—who thought nothing of telling the president how to run the country—gave him a letter warning against making the war a crusade against slavery. "Neither confiscation of property . . . [n]or forcible abolition of slavery should be contemplated for a moment,"[115] said McClellan. Two months later, McClellan won the victory that enabled Lincoln to ignore his "advice.")

On September 22, 1862, Lincoln opened his cabinet meeting by reading from a book of humorous stories. Then, growing serious, he spoke about the Emancipation Proclamation. "I think the time has come," said the president. "I wish it were a better time. I wish that we were in a better condition. The action of the army against the rebels has not been quite what I should have best liked."[116]

Nevertheless, Antietam was a Union victory, and Lincoln was determined not to squander the opportunity. At the meeting, he again read the document, which would take effect on January 1, 1863. The cabinet made a few minor changes in wording, Montgomery Blair again wor-

ried about the effect on the border states, and that was it: A document that would come to be considered one of the great state papers in U.S. history was ready to be issued.

Two days later, on Monday, September 24, the "preliminary" Emancipation Proclamation was published. Suddenly all America—as well as the world—knew that the president who had tried for so long to steer a moderate course on slavery had irrevocably come down on the side of abolition.

In celebration, a brass band came to the White House to serenade Lincoln on this memorable day. The president addressed them from a balcony: "I can only trust in God I have made no mistake. It is now for the country and the world to pass judgment on it, and, may be, take action upon it."[117]

An Act of Immense Consequence

That judgment was quick in coming. Antislavery forces hailed the document. "We shout for joy that we live to record this righteous decree,"[118] said Frederick Douglass. Others called it an act of immense historic consequence.

However, Democrats and pro-slavery advocates denounced the proclamation. Former Democratic president of the United States Franklin Pierce said the proclamation proved that Lincoln, "to the extent of his limited ability and narrow intelligence,"[119] was an abolitionist tool. Another critic said that the proclamation made it impossible for "patriotic"

Lincoln and his cabinet review the preliminary Emancipation Proclamation. The document was hailed by antislavery forces.

Americans to hope for a Union victory and claimed that the Confederacy was closer to the spirit of the founding fathers than was the government of "Abraham Africanus I." Even the legislature of Lincoln's own state of Illinois attacked the proclamation, claiming that it turned a war for the vindication of the U.S. Constitution into a crusade for the liberation of millions of slaves.

Predictably, the South erupted in anger over the Emancipation Proclamation. To them, the document was an open invitation for slaves to begin killing, burning, raping, and looting at will. Confederate president Jefferson Davis called it "the most execrable measure recorded in the history of guilty man,"[120] while the Richmond newspaper *Enquirer* raged, "What

shall we call him [Lincoln]? Coward, assassin, savage, murderer of women and babies? Or shall we consider them all as embodied in the word fiend, and call him Lincoln, the Fiend?"[121]

One of the president's greatest concerns was the Union armed forces' reaction to the proclamation. Although some soldiers were abolitionists, the majority had gone to war to preserve the Union; Lincoln wondered if they would still fight if they knew that now they were also fighting to free the slaves.

Fortunately, even though some Union generals, like McClellan, disagreed with the proclamation, the rank-and-file soldier recognized that, by freeing the slaves, Lincoln was dealing a crippling blow to the enemy. Typical of many soldiers' opinions was that expressed by an Indiana colonel who said that destroying anything that gave the rebels strength was good. "The army will sustain the emancipation proclamation and enforce it with the bayonet,"[122] he said.

By issuing the preliminary Emancipation Proclamation, Lincoln had come full circle from the president who told the South at his inauguration that he had no intention of interfering with slavery where

George McClellan

A strange mixture of superb organizer and reluctant warrior, George McClellan shepherded the Union army through some of its darkest hours, yet he threw away a golden opportunity to win the war.

Born in Philadelphia on December 3, 1826, McClellan graduated second in his class at West Point, served with distinction in the Mexican War, and was an engineer, author, and general when Lincoln in desperation put him in charge of the Northern army after it had been routed at the first battle of Bull Run. Supposedly able to bend a quarter between his thumb and forefinger, McClellan immediately brought much-needed discipline and structure to the thousands of green recruits who poured into the army encampment.

But if organization was his forte, fighting was not. Always a cautious man, McClellan constantly imagined that the smaller Confederate army he was facing outnumbered his in strength by a wide margin, and he incessantly besieged Washington for reinforcements. Finally, in September 1862 came the type of luck that every general prays for: Union troops found a copy of Robert E. Lee's special orders, and McClellan knew virtually the entire Southern battle plan. Even with this incredible advantage, however, McClellan waited too long; the Battle of Antietam that resulted, instead of possibly being a decisive victory, was merely a bloody stalemate that was considered a Union triumph only because Lee retreated. Soon after this, tired of urging McClellan to fight aggressively, Lincoln replaced him.

In 1864 McClellan was the Democratic candidate for president, but he lost to Lincoln. He later served as governor of New Jersey from 1878 to 1881. He died in 1885.

Lincoln replaced George McClellan (pictured) because of the general's reluctance to commit his troops in battle.

it already existed. The difference was, of course, the war; two years of bloody struggle, of death on a massive and incomprehensible scale with no end in sight, had changed how Lincoln viewed the war. The man who had begun by trying to tread lightly on the Confederacy was now saying that, once the final Emancipation Proclamation was issued, the war would become one of subjugation in which the aim was to destroy the South and slavery, and replace it with new ideas.

Yet the president's actions are understandable when the context of why he issued the proclamation is considered. Lincoln freed the slaves as part of his duties as the commander in chief of a nation involved in a devastating civil war. Acting under his war powers to destroy the resources of an enemy was a far cry from Lincoln's freeing the slaves as a matter of domestic policy. This sudden strike at one of the key props upholding the Confederacy was the hidden strength underlying the Emancipation Proclamation, and what made it acceptable to so many people who had grown weary of the war, no matter what their views on slavery.

As the final months of 1862 passed, there was speculation that Lincoln would back down and not issue the final proclamation on January 1, 1863. The whole country began wondering about the president's intentions.

Meanwhile, the Democratic Party vigorously attacked the preliminary Emancipation Proclamation, hoping to score a big victory in the fall 1862 elections. With a slogan of "The Union as it was and the Constitution as it is," the Democrats did indeed score impressive victories in elections in New York, Illinois, Indiana, and New Jersey; as a result, the number of Democratic congressmen leaped from forty-four to seventy-five, and many prominent Republicans were defeated. Fortunately for Lincoln, the border states of Kentucky, Maryland, and Missouri, plus the new state of West Virginia, elected enough Republican congressmen to keep the party's majority intact.

Election Fuels Speculation

The election results further fueled speculation that Lincoln would not issue the final Emancipation Proclamation on January 1. Proclaiming that abolition had been "slaughtered," gleeful Democrats introduced a congressional resolution calling emancipation a high crime against the Constitution.

Lincoln himself added to the uncertainty surrounding the Emancipation Proclamation when he addressed Congress on December 1. Once again, he urged that they adopt his plan for gradual, compensated emancipation, as well as colonization for freed slaves. He also proposed a constitutional amendment that would compensate every state that banned slavery before January 1, 1900.

Both anti- and pro-slavery groups tried to read into the president's words, seeking clues as to whether or not he would issue the Emancipation Proclamation. Some abolitionists considered sending delegations to visit the president to bolster his courage; others proclaimed their faith in Lincoln. Emancipation foes, on the other hand, felt certain that Lincoln would not attack "property" worth millions of dollars, and also unleash a spasm of murder and arson by freed slaves, by issuing the proclamation.

Further adding to the confusion was low Union morale. With the military and political situations both bleak, rumors were rife that Lincoln would resign in favor of Vice President Hannibal Hamlin and also that General McClellan, recently deposed as head of the Union armies, would be called back to Washington to assume dictatorial powers.

The watching, waiting, and wondering reached a fever pitch on December 31. In many cities, groups of whites and blacks gathered to wait for word that the document had been signed so that they could offer prayers of thanksgiving. Several prominent abolitionists, among them Frederick Douglass and William Lloyd Garrison, met at Tremont Temple in Boston. Throughout the nation, anticipation and anxiety hung heavy in the air as people waited to see what the first day of the new year would bring.

On January 1, 1863, the president spent several hours at a New Year's Day reception at the White House. Later that afternoon, Secretary of State Seward and his son Fred arrived at the executive mansion, where

William Lloyd Garrison met with fellow abolitionists at Tremont Temple in Boston to await the signing of the Emancipation Proclamation.

they found Lincoln alone in his office, the Emancipation Proclamation spread out before him on his desk.

"I never, in my life, felt more certain that I was doing right, than I do in signing this paper,"[123] said the president. He mentioned how stiff his arm was from shaking hands at the reception and how, if that caused his hand to shake and his signature to be less than bold, future generations would say he had second thoughts about signing the document.

But the firm, clear "Abraham Lincoln" that he signed the proclamation with left little doubt about his intentions, as if the words themselves were not clear enough: "I do order and declare that all persons held as slaves within said designated States, and parts of States, are, and henceforward shall be free."[124]

(Although it is commonly thought that the Emancipation Proclamation ended slavery in the United States, in reality it applied only to the states or parts of states that were in rebellion. In other areas—all the Union states, the border states, Tennessee, and parts of Louisiana and Virginia held by the North—it had no effect.)

Concerned that the proclamation would trigger a destructive rampage by slaves, the document urged freed slaves to abstain from violence. It also authorized the use of black troops and sailors in the Union armed forces.

Reaction to the "final" Emancipation Proclamation was similar to that which greeted the preliminary version in September. Antislavery advocates were overjoyed; celebrations, including the booming of a hundred guns, broke out in cities such as Boston, Buffalo, and Pittsburgh. Such revelries continued throughout the night, and many blacks and whites greeted the dawn of the new day together with tearful prayers. "A great day,"

wrote Longfellow of that historic New Year's Day. "A beautiful day, full of sunshine, ending in a tranquil moonlight night. May it be symbolic."[125]

By the same token, those who had criticized the document in September again attacked it. "While the Proclamation leaves slavery untouched where his decree can be enforced, he emancipates slaves where his decree cannot be enforced," said the New York *Herald* newspaper. "Friends of human rights will be at a loss to understand this discrimination."[126]

The Richmond newspaper *Examiner* called the document "the most startling political crime, the most stupid political

A Union soldier and a black family rejoice at the news of the signing of the Emancipation Proclamation.

blunder, yet known in American history."[127]

The reaction of Confederate president Jefferson Davis was even harsher. On January 12, 1863, Davis declared that all free blacks captured and all free blacks in the South would be made slaves. He also threatened to turn over all captured Union officers to state governments for punishment, calling them criminals engaged in inciting servile insurrection.

No Recognition for Confederacy

Lincoln received more favorable news from Union diplomats in London. The Emancipation Proclamation had stopped any movement by the British government to recognize the Confederacy. "The Emancipation Proclamation has done more for us here than all our former victories and all our diplomacy,"[128] wrote Henry Adams from the British capital.

On January 8, 1863, Lincoln explained why he had chosen this time to move against slavery:

After the commencement of hostilities, I struggled nearly a year and a half to get along without touching the "institution" [slavery]; and when finally I conditionally determined to touch it, I gave a hundred days fair notice of any purpose, to all the States and people, within which time they could have turned it wholly aside, by simply again becoming good citizens of the United States. They chose to disregard it, and I made the peremptory proclamation on what appeared to me to be a military necessity.[129]

In future years, historians would debate whether Lincoln truly freed the slaves with this historic document or whether the slaves freed themselves by escaping and pouring into Union army camps in such numbers that it became obvious that emancipation would mortally wound the Confederacy.

But what mattered at the time was that Abraham Lincoln had struck a huge blow at the Confederacy's ability to wage war, while at the same time moving the nation one giant step closer to its founding principle that all men are created equal.

Chapter 6

The End of a Long, Bloody Road

The Emancipation Proclamation represented a radical change in Lincoln's slavery policy. For those who accused him of changing his mind on the subject, the president had a ready answer: "Yes, I have. And I don't think much of a man who is not wiser today than he was yesterday." [130]

By issuing the Emancipation Proclamation, Lincoln proved that he had indeed grown wiser. He had learned that the limited war he initially hoped to fight to suppress the rebellion was not enough. By the summer of 1862 he knew that victory required total warfare, with the North using all the weapons at its command to strike at every Confederate resource. By freeing the slaves, Lincoln had attacked one of the Confederacy's key advantages. Now, thanks to the Emancipation Proclamation, the North was about to unleash another weapon on the Confederacy: black troops.

Abolitionist leaders like Frederick Douglass had urged the North to use black soldiers for some time. But even though blacks had served proudly in the American Revolution and the War of 1812, they had not been allowed to enroll in the Union army.

The seas, however, followed different rules. Blacks were permitted in the Union navy from the beginning of the war, and they had ably served as firemen, coal shovelers, cooks, and stewards. They had also proven that they could assume higher roles when necessary. William Tillman, a black steward on a Union merchant vessel captured by Confederates, killed all the Southern officers aboard ship and sailed her straight to New York. In another instance, a slave pilot named Robert Smalls hijacked a Confederate gunboat from Charleston Harbor; with only a slave crew and their families to help him, he piloted the ship past Confederate batteries and into Union waters.

Pointing to acts of heroism such as these, Douglass and others pressed for the use of black troops as a way to help blacks gain equality with whites:

Blacks were allowed to join the navy from the beginning of the Civil War.

Once let the black man get upon his person the brass letters, U.S.; let him get an eagle on his buttons, and a musket on his shoulder and bullets in his pocket, and there is no power on earth which can deny that he has earned the right to citizenship in the United States.[131]

Complicating the use of black soldiers, however, was the Confederacy's attitude toward them. The rebels refused to consider captured black soldiers as legitimate prisoners of war; any black who fell into the hands of the Confederates could almost certainly expect death. "We ought never to be inconvenienced with such prisoners [blacks]," said Confederate secretary of war James Seddon, who recommended "summary execution on those taken."[132]

Knowing that black troops faced inhumane treatment if captured, Union authorities hesitated to use them in combat. Once the Emancipation Proclamation was issued, however, the movement to recruit blacks became too powerful to resist. Douglass and other abolitionists began assembling black regiments to fight for the Union.

The act of whites arming blacks to fight whites had an unreal quality about it. "Saw the first regiment of blacks march through Beach Street," wrote Longfellow in Boston in May 1863. "An imposing sight, with something wild and strange about it, like a dream."[133]

Even Lincoln, who had earlier rejected the idea of black soldiers because of fear of the country's reaction, became enthusiastic over it. "The bare sight of fifty thousand armed, and drilled black soldiers on the banks of the Mississippi, would end the rebellion at once,"[134] he said in March 1863.

Ultimately, about 186,000 blacks joined the Union army and formed 166 units,

some of which distinguished themselves in combat. One of these was the 54th Massachusetts Infantry. On July 18, 1863, the 54th Massachusetts—in which both of Douglass's sons served—led a desperate attack against well-entrenched Confederates holding Fort Wagner in Charleston Harbor. Although the 54th lost nearly half its men, including its white commander, Robert Gould Shaw, the soldiers managed to reach the fort's

The 54th Massachusetts Infantry charges Fort Wagner. This valiant act helped to demonstrate "the manhood of the colored race."

parapet and hold it for nearly an hour before finally retreating in the face of withering Confederate fire. This valiant attack received widespread publicity in the North and helped to change perceptions about blacks. "Through the cannon smoke of that dark night," said the *Atlantic Monthly*, "the manhood of the colored race shines before many eyes that would not see."[135] Four members of the 54th Massachusetts received the Gilmore Medal for bravery during the Fort Wagner assault.

The Fort Pillow Atrocities

Sadly, the atrocities that Union authorities feared were indeed inflicted on black soldiers. Many of those captured were killed, often in gruesome ways that went beyond the bounds of even this bloody war. Perhaps the most glaring example was at Fort Pillow, Tennessee, in April 1864. Outnumbering the six hundred Union defenders ten to one, Confederate troops under General Nathan Bedford Forrest easily captured the fort. Then, after the battle was over, the Southerners systematically killed as many as three hundred of the fort's defenders—most of them black. According to a congressional committee investigating the charges, "Men, women, even children, were shot down, beaten, hacked with sabers; children not more than ten years old were forced to stand up and face their murderers while being shot; sick and wounded were butchered without mercy."[136]

Forrest did not bother to deny the massacre. "The river was dyed with the blood of the slaughtered for 200 yards," he said. "It is hoped that these facts will demonstrate to the northern people that negro soldiers cannot cope with Southerners."[137]

Despite the knowledge that they might meet a similar fate, blacks continued to enlist in, fight for, and die for the Union. At the end of the war, more than thirty-eight thousand blacks had been killed. Approximately 85 percent of blacks eligible to fight enlisted in the Union army. The value of black troops was endorsed by General Grant, who called them "a powerful ally" and "the heaviest blow yet given the Confederacy."[138]

But, examples set by black troops not withstanding, racial attitudes and opinions changed very slowly. Slavery continued to exist in areas not affected by the Emancipation Proclamation, and racial equality remained a volatile issue in both North and South.

The Democratic Party continued to be an instigator of social unrest. Its blistering assaults against emancipation were bolstered by another emotional issue in the spring of 1863—the draft, which passed in Congress almost exclusively through Republican support. Democrats used both the draft and emancipation to attack the Lincoln administration. "We will not render support to the present Administration in its wicked Abolition crusade [and] we will resist to the death all attempts to draft any of our citizens into the army,"[139] pledged a group of Midwestern Democrats.

Inequities for Black Troops

Finally given their opportunity to join the Union army through Lincoln's Emancipation Proclamation, blacks rushed to enlist. Unfortunately, military life for blacks carried the same prejudices and inequities that civilian life did.

Although they wanted to fight, black regiments were often relegated to the most menial tasks, such as digging trenches. Almost all of the officers were white; no black soldier was allowed to rise above the rank of captain. Black privates were also paid just $10 per month, as compared to $13 for whites. In protest, some black regiments served without pay rather than receive less than whites.

Other inequities suffered by black troops included not receiving a clothing allowance, like whites did, and having difficulties finding doctors to serve them and treat their wounds and illnesses.

Yet despite all the hardships, black soldiers fought bravely and valiantly whenever given the opportunity. By war's end, approximately 186,000 blacks proudly wore Union blue.

One of the 186,000 blacks who, despite the hardships, proudly wore Union blue.

On July 13, 1863, the two combustible ingredients of emancipation and the draft came together and exploded into violence in New York City. A mob inflamed by Democratic rhetoric about the draft began rioting; the focus of the violence quickly shifted to blacks, because it was feared they were poised to take the jobs vacated by those who were drafted. For four days a large mob raged out of control in the city, hunting down and killing blacks; burning a black orphanage, a black church, and black boardinghouses; and battling police. Only the intervention of the Union army restored order.

Oddly, the New York draft riot helped turn the tide of public opinion in favor of blacks. Just after the riot came news of the heroism of the 54th Massachusetts at Fort Wagner, and the contrast was obvious: Black soldiers were fighting and dying to save the Union, while lawless whites threatened to destroy it.

Mobs of whites set fire to black boardinghouses during the New York City draft riot. The riot helped turn the tide of public opinion in favor of blacks.

In August, with memories of the riot still strong throughout the country, Lincoln publicly chided Democrats.

You are dissatisfied with me about the negro. But some of the commanders of our armies in the field . . . believe the emancipation policy, and the use of colored troops, constitute the heaviest blow yet dealt to the rebellion. You say you will not fight to free negroes. Some of them seem willing to fight for you.[140]

The president's remarks, along with the growing realization that emancipation

was aiding the Union war effort, helped turn public opinion against slavery. In the autumn 1863 elections, Republicans who had been worried about emancipation as a campaign issue just a few months before linked it with patriotism and scored impressive victories over the Democrats. The party's strong electoral showing (including garnering 94 percent of the absentee soldier vote) was a clear sign that people were now supporting emancipation.

"The change of opinion on this slavery question . . . is a great and historic fact," said a New York Republican after the election. "Who could have predicted . . . this great and blessed revolution?"[141]

One month later, during his annual congressional message, Lincoln agreed that the storm over emancipation was clearing. He told the members that, although the Emancipation Proclamation had been followed by dark and doubtful days, the crisis that seemed imminent had now passed.

The president also rejected any efforts to revoke or alter the Emancipation Proclamation. "While I remain in my present position I shall not attempt to retract or modify the emancipation proclamation; nor shall I return to slavery any person who is free by the terms of that proclamation, or by any of the acts of Congress."[142]

The president who spoke these words was a far different man than the one who had come to Washington just three years earlier. By the beginning of 1864 Lincoln was exhausted, ground down by the disputes over slavery, the relentless pressure of the war, the constant crush of favor-seekers, the personal trials he had endured, and the countless other duties of the presidency. "Rest," he said. "I suppose it is good for the body. But the tired part of me is *inside* and out of reach."[143]

The duties of the office, once so appealing to Lincoln, had turned into bone-wearying tedium. When a visitor asked him how he liked being president, Lincoln replied by telling a story about a man who was tarred and feathered and ridden out of town on a rail. If it wasn't for the honor of the thing, the man said, he would much rather have walked. That, Lincoln concluded, was how he felt about the presidency.

Still, early in 1864, the dark clouds over the White House seemed to be lifting. The Confederate forces appeared on the verge of defeat, thanks to competent generals such as Ulysses S. Grant and William T. Sherman leading the Union armies. Emancipation was also being accepted by more and more Northerners.

A Constitutional Amendment

With the war in capable hands, Lincoln turned his attention to a constitutional amendment banning slavery. Some states had already taken the lead: In 1863 West Virginia adopted a constitution that provided gradual emancipation, and in that same year both Missouri and Tennessee initiated similar measures. The following year, Maryland abolished slavery.

Lincoln found his match for Robert E. Lee in generals Ulysses S. Grant (above) and William T. Sherman (below).

those states, that returned to federal control. Republicans worried that governments in these areas might be dominated by conservative elements of the old planters' aristocracy that would either try to revive slavery or else delay eliminating it. A constitutional amendment abolishing slavery throughout the United States would permanently end this threat.

The Thirteenth Amendment

When the Thirteenth Amendment to the Constitution, abolishing slavery, was introduced in Congress early in 1864, it seemed as if it would quickly be approved. The measure easily gained the necessary two-thirds majority in the Senate, passing on April 8 by a vote of thirty-eight to six.

In the House of Representatives, however, it was a different story. One obstacle was that the amendment did not offer compensation to slaveholders; some representatives argued that the government should not take this "property" without offering something in return. Another problem was that some legislators thought it should be up to the states to end slavery, rather than the federal government. A third objection was that such a portentous change in the country's social and economic structure should not be made without the participation of the eleven seceded states.

Proponents of the amendment argued strenuously for its passage, pointing out that this was a chance to forever end the evil that had brought such misery to

What made the idea of a constitutional amendment appealing was that it would provide a solution to the problem of how to deal with seceded states, or portions of the country. But on June 15, the amendment fell thirteen votes short of a two-thirds majority in the House, passing by a count of ninety-three to sixty-five.

By the time of that vote, however, the atmosphere in the North had changed dramatically. The optimism of early spring that the war may be ending had withered by midsummer. With Grant unable to bludgeon Lee into submission in the East, and Sherman also stalled in the West, the war seemed more hopeless than ever. Mounting casualty lists caused a deep defeatist gloom to settle over the war-weary Union. "The people are wild for peace,"[144] wrote Republican politician Thurlow Weed.

In a letter to the president, Horace Greeley eloquently summed up the nation's mood during that dark summer of 1864: "Our bleeding, bankrupt, almost dying country longs for peace—shudders at the prospect of fresh conscriptions, of further wholesale devastations, and of new rivers of human blood."[145]

With Northern morale rapidly ebbing, Greeley became involved in peace negotiations with Confederate representatives in Canada. Lincoln had set restoration of the Union and the cessation of slavery as his terms for ending the war, but when negotiations collapsed, Democrats and others pointed to emancipation as the sole stumbling block to peace. (In reality, Jefferson Davis had long made it clear that the South's goal was either independence or extermination.) Pressure mounted on Lincoln, even from Republican leaders, to make restoration of the Union the sole condition for ending the war.

Horace Greeley

One of the most influential public figures during this era was newspaper editor Horace Greeley, a man whose opinions and emotions changed with each new wind.

Born in New Hampshire on February 3, 1811, Greeley came to New York City in 1831. After editing various publications and gaining a reputation as a political writer, Greeley founded the *New York Tribune* newspaper in 1841 to promote the Whig Party with a low-cost publication. The paper was immediately successful, and Greeley remained its editor for over three decades. The paper became so influential that when he advised a young clergyman seeking a new start in life to "Go west, young man," an entire generation listened.

Although not an abolitionist, Greeley was a fierce opponent of slavery. He was an influential figure in the Republican Party, and he frequently peppered the pages of the *Tribune* with advice to party leaders, including Lincoln. Yet this advice was often contradictory; within days, he went from urging federal troops to march on Richmond to urging President Lincoln that the war be abandoned after the first defeat at Bull Run.

In later years he continued to follow his heart, no matter where it led him; the staunch Union supporter even signed a bail bond for Jefferson Davis after the war because he thought the former Confederate president's long imprisonment was a constitutional rights violation. In 1872, disillusioned with the Republicans, Greeley ran against incumbent Republican president Ulysses Grant on the Liberal Republican ticket. Greeley lost the election, and died soon afterward.

With emancipation facing its biggest test since the Emancipation Proclamation, the president went on the offensive. Publicly, he told Republicans that, while the only reason for the war was to restore the Union, "No human power can subdue this rebellion without using the Emancipation lever as I have done." He spoke of the black soldiers fighting and dying for the Union and how they were risking their lives because of their burning desire to be free. "And the promise being made, must be kept," said the president. "The world shall know that I will keep my faith to my friends & enemies, come what will." [146]

Privately, however, the relentless pressure to end the war made him retreat from his strong public stance. Lincoln knew that some Republicans were searching for an alternative candidate for the November 1864 presidential election, certain that he couldn't win. Even Lincoln himself, when despair over the stagnant military situation had reached its lowest ebb in late August, had written that he probably would not be reelected.

Thus the temptation to waver slightly on emancipation was too much to resist, even for Lincoln. In a letter to a Northern Democrat about peace negotiations, he wrote, "If Jefferson Davis wishes to know what I would do if he were to offer peace and re-union, saying nothing about slavery, let him try me." To Henry Raymond, chairman of the Republican National Committee, Lincoln went even farther. He wrote instructions for Raymond to go to Richmond as a special negotiator, to propose that "upon the restoration of the Union and the national authority, the war shall cease at once, all remaining questions [including slavery] to be left for adjustment by peaceful modes." [147]

Staring into the abyss of a full-scale retreat on emancipation, Lincoln abruptly turned away. He neither dispatched Raymond to Richmond nor sent the "try me" letter. Emancipation remained a Union condition for ending the war.

"Wiped Off the Earth"

One week later, on September 2, 1864, Sherman's army captured Atlanta, and the entire military situation improved dramatically for the Union. Suddenly there was nothing to stop Sherman from sweeping north to Virginia and trapping Lee's army between his own forces and those of Grant. The South, which only weeks before had been confidently anticipating that after the election there would be a new president who would be willing to negotiate a settlement of the war, was overcome with the same despair that had recently gripped the North. "Since Atlanta I have felt as if all were dead within me, forever," wrote Mary Boykin Chestnut of South Carolina. "We are going to be wiped off the earth." [148]

The presidential election brought more bad news for the South. Lincoln won a resounding victory over his Democratic challenger, former Union general George McClellan. Lincoln won every

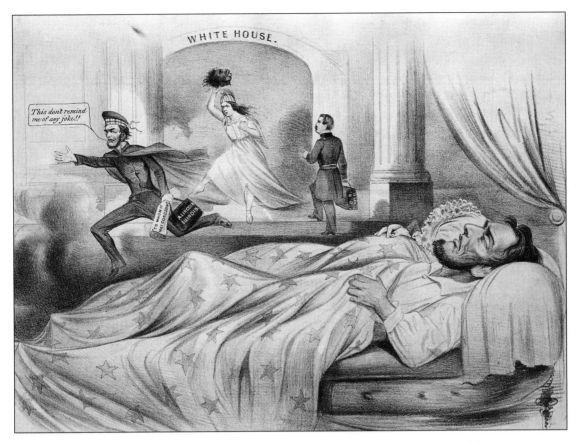

In this cartoon, Lincoln has a nightmare that he loses the White House to George McClellan.

state but Kentucky, Delaware, and New Jersey, giving him an overwhelming Electoral College victory of 212 to 21. Lincoln's win destroyed the South's last hope that the Union would renounce emancipation as a condition for ending the war. Even the most optimistic Southerner could see defeat staring him in the face.

In December, the president, flush with success over his election victory, urged Congress to reconsider passing the Thirteenth Amendment to the Constitution abolishing slavery. In the next Congress, Lincoln pointed out, Republicans would have a three-quarters majority in the House of Representatives and could easily pass it then; by doing it now, said the president, this important amendment would go down in history as a bipartisan achievement.

Faced with this inevitability, the Democrats again balked. Some of the same arguments that had defeated the amendment the first time were repeated, along with some new ones. Perhaps the most intriguing was that it was pointed out that, when the Constitution was written, slave states outnumbered free states and had it in their power to force slavery on the entire nation. Now that the tables were turned, said some, it wasn't right that the free states were forcing their will on the slave states.

Since logic wasn't working, the Lincoln administration resorted to patronage to get the amendment passed. Approximately one dozen lame-duck Democratic congressmen (those whose terms expired in March, when the new Congress took over) were promised political favors in exchange for their support of the amendment.

Even with all of this political wheeling and dealing, the outcome was still in doubt when the House of Representatives met on January 31, 1865, to consider the amendment. The debate went on for hours, while the galleries swelled to capacity; most of the Senate and the Supreme Court were also in attendance. When the votes were finally counted, the amendment passed, 119 to 56. Sixteen of the eighty House Democrats (fourteen of whom were lame ducks) had voted affirmative.

When the vote was announced, the House erupted into thunderous applause. For ten minutes, women waved handkerchiefs, men shook hands and slapped each other on the back, and people stood on their seats and cheered. Outside, a hundred-gun salute was fired. In honor of the occasion, the House adjourned for the remainder of the day.

Thus slavery was finally abolished throughout the United States. Although the amendment still needed to be ratified by three-fourths of the states, the number of Republican-controlled state governments made that little more than a formality. (Eight states ratified the amendment within the first week. It was ratified on December 6, 1865.)

Copperheads

Primarily made up of Northern Democrats who were opposed to the war and the policies of the Lincoln administration, copperheads gave the South false hope that the North would eventually tire of the war and give up fighting.

Although where the name came from is uncertain—some said it referred to the venomous snake, whereas others said that it referred to little copper buttons depicting the head of Lady Liberty that they cut from pennies and wore on their lapels—the copperheads' political position was quite clear. Instead of war with the South, copperheads called for compromise (although not all were pro-slavery). They also vigorously fought Lincoln on many other domestic matters, such as the administration's decision to suspend habeas corpus (thus enabling people to be jailed without being brought before a judge or jury).

Despite their often-sincere convictions, copperheads probably hurt the Union war effort by telling the Confederacy that Northern antiwar fervor was greater than what really existed. There were also concerns that copperhead groups were plotting to take control of various Northern states and negotiate a separate peace with the Confederacy. All these fears, however, proved groundless.

The House of Representatives erupts in applause and celebration after passing the amendment to the Constitution that abolished slaverly in the United States.

Lincoln was delighted by the vote. The amendment, he said, was "a King's cure for all evils. It winds the whole thing up."[149]

Others were more effusive in their praise, both for the amendment and the president. "To whom is the country more immediately indebted for this vital and saving amendment of the Constitution than, perhaps, to any other man?" wrote William Lloyd Garrison. "I believe I may confidently answer—to the humble rail-splitter of Illinois—to the Presidential chainbreaker for millions of the oppressed—to Abraham Lincoln!"[150]

Anyone who doubted that the passage of the Thirteenth Amendment was going to result in a radical new order in America had only to look as far as the U.S. Supreme Court. On February 1, the day after the amendment was approved by the House of Representatives, abolitionist senator Charles Sumner presented Boston lawyer John Rock for admission to practice before the highest court in the land. Rock was immediately sworn in—the first black accredited to the Supreme Court, which just eight years earlier, in the *Dred Scott* decision, had denied citizenship rights to slaves.

Thanks to Abraham Lincoln and the abolition of slavery, the country had indeed embarked on a "new birth of freedom."

Out of the Ashes

By the time the Thirteenth Amendment passed the House of Representatives, the Confederacy was in its final months. While in the West Sherman had swept aside all opposition and was racing northward, Grant's persistent attacks on Lee's gallant Army of Northern Virginia had drained it of vital men and materials.

Near the end, the South tried two desperate gambles to reverse the tide: arming slaves as troops (despite the protests of Confederate officers, one of whom pointedly noted, "If slaves seem good soldiers, then our whole theory of slavery is wrong"[151]) and offering to abolish slavery in return for diplomatic recognition by Great Britain. Both were too little, too late; the Confederacy was dying, and nothing could save it.

Nothing could save slavery either. It was not only the constitutional amendment but the Union armies that applied the final blow to the institution that had long bedeviled the United States; they roared through the South, destroying plantations and leaving huge contingents of former slaves in their wake. "The whole army of the United States could not restore the institution of slavery in the South," observed General Sherman. "They can't get back their slaves, any more than they can get back their dead grandfathers. It is dead."[152]

On April 2, 1865, the Confederate government fled from Richmond just ahead of the rapidly approaching Union forces. Two days later, saying "Thank God I have lived to see this,"[153] Abraham Lincoln visited Richmond. As he walked the streets of the burning city, the president was besieged by grateful blacks, who wept with joy and strained just to touch the clothing of the "Great Emancipator."

Lee Surrenders

On April 9, 1865, Lee surrendered to Grant at Appomattox Court House in Virginia,

On April 4, 1865, Lincoln toured the ruins of Richmond (pictured). The Civil War officially ended five days later.

effectively ending the Civil War. Unable to stand the thought of living in the restored Union, ardent secessionist Edmund Ruffin, who had fired one of the first shots at Fort Sumter to begin the war, killed himself.

Five days later, on Good Friday, after telling his wife during an afternoon carriage ride that they must both be more cheerful in the future, Lincoln and Mary attended an evening performance of the play *Our American Cousin* at Ford's Theatre in Washington, D.C. While watching the play, Lincoln was shot in the back of the head by John Wilkes Booth, an actor and embittered supporter of the Confederacy. Lincoln died the following morning—April 15, 1865.

With the death of Lincoln went millions of freed slaves' best hope for a chance to achieve equality with whites. Among all of the influential figures in the United States at the end of the Civil War, only Lincoln had the respect, ability, and political wisdom to bring blacks into the mainstream of American society.

With Lincoln removed, radical Republicans in Congress were free to punish the South for the war, through a vindictive program known as Reconstruction.

While watching a play at Ford's Theatre in Washington, D.C., Lincoln was shot by John Wilkes Booth.

Democrats of the slavery days were back in power in every state in the South. For Southern blacks, it was as if the Civil War had never been fought.

Beginning around 1890, Southern states started enacting "Jim Crow" segregation laws that established two separate societies—one for whites and one for blacks. In 1896 the U.S. Supreme Court gave its legal blessing to segregation, ruling in *Plessy v. Ferguson* that "separate but equal" facilities (restaurants, schools, etc.) did not violate "equal protection under the laws" as guaranteed by the Fourteenth Amendment to the U.S. Constitution.

For over half a century, "separate but equal" was the unofficial law of the land, particularly in the South. Finally, in 1954, the Supreme Court ruled in the case of *Brown v. Board of Education* that school segregation was illegal. This began a series of civil rights actions by blacks demanding equality. Finally, in 1964—one hundred years after the Civil War was fought—Congress passed the landmark Civil Rights Act to enforce the rights guaranteed by the Fourteenth Amendment. It had taken nearly a century, but the process begun by Abraham Lincoln and the abolition of slavery had finally been completed.

In turn, the governments of Southern states were free to take out their anger and frustration over the loss of the war, and the humiliation of Reconstruction, on freed blacks. Without any skills, many blacks went back to their former masters to earn a living and wound up working in situations very similar to slavery. In fact, despite laws and other constitutional amendments guaranteeing them citizenship and voting rights, blacks had little political power in the South—if they were even allowed to participate in the process. Roving gangs of hoodlums and organized secret societies like the Ku Klux Klan instilled terror in blacks with threats, violence, and murder. By 1876 the old-line

✭ Notes ✭

Introduction: Too Raw a Wound

1. Quoted in John Hope Franklin and Alfred A. Moss Jr., *From Slavery to Freedom*. New York: McGraw-Hill, 1988, p. 67.
2. Quoted in Franklin and Moss, *From Slavery to Freedom*, p. 67.

Chapter 1: The Man from Illinois

3. Quoted in Michael Burlingame, *The Inner World of Abraham Lincoln*. Urbana: University of Illinois Press, 1994, p. 38.
4. Quoted in Burlingame, *The Inner World of Abraham Lincoln*, p. 39.
5. Quoted in Burlingame, *The Inner World of Abraham Lincoln*, p. 41.
6. Burlingame, *The Inner World of Abraham Lincoln*, p. 42.
7. Quoted in Burlingame, *The Inner World of Abraham Lincoln*, p. 22.
8. Quoted in Burlingame, *The Inner World of Abraham Lincoln*, p. 22.
9. Quoted in William Hanchett, *Out of the Wilderness: The Life of Abraham Lincoln*. Urbana: University of Illinois Press, 1994, p. 12.
10. Quoted in Carl Sandburg, *Abraham Lincoln: The Prairie Years and the War Years*. New York: Harcourt, Brace, 1954, p. 49.
11. Quoted in Sandburg, *Abraham Lincoln*, p. 49.
12. Quoted in Burlingame, *The Inner World of Abraham Lincoln*, p. 25.
13. Quoted in Hanchett, *Out of the Wilderness*, p. 32.
14. Quoted in Hanchett, *Out of the Wilderness*, p. 40.
15. Quoted in Sandburg, *Abraham Lincoln*, p. 109.
16. Quoted in Burlingame, *The Inner World of Abraham Lincoln*, p. 242.
17. Quoted in Burlingame, *The Inner World of Abraham Lincoln*, p. 1.
18. Burlingame, *The Inner World of Abraham Lincoln*, p. 5.
19. Quoted in Burlingame, *The Inner World of Abraham Lincoln*, p. 5.
20. Quoted in Geoffrey C. Ward, *The Civil War: An Illustrated History*. New York: Knopf, 1990, p. 20.
21. Quoted in Burlingame, *The Inner World of Abraham Lincoln*, p. 30.
22. Quoted in Burlingame, *The Inner World of Abraham Lincoln*, p. 33.
23. Quoted in Sandburg, *Abraham Lincoln*, p. 122.
24. Quoted in Sandburg, *Abraham Lincoln*, p. 138.
25. Quoted in James M. McPherson, *Battle*

Cry of Freedom. New York: Oxford University Press, 1988, p. 184.

26. Quoted in McPherson, *Battle Cry of Freedom,* p. 186.

27. Quoted in James M. McPherson, *Abraham Lincoln and the Second American Revolution.* New York: Oxford University Press, 1990, p. 126.

28. Quoted in Sandburg, *Abraham Lincoln,* p. 144.

Chapter 2: The South and Slavery

29. Quoted in Ward, *The Civil War,* p. 8.

30. Quoted in Bruce Levine, *Half Slave and Half Free.* New York: Hill and Wang, 1992, p. 106.

31. Quoted in McPherson, *Battle Cry of Freedom,* p. 56.

32. Quoted in Levine, *Half Slave and Half Free,* p. 160.

33. Quoted in Bruce Catton, *The American Heritage Picture History of the Civil War.* New York: American Heritage/ Bonanza Books, 1960, p. 10.

34. Quoted in Levine, *Half Slave and Half Free,* p. 160.

35. Quoted in Ward, *The Civil War,* p. 14.

36. Quoted in Ward, *The Civil War,* p. 14.

37. Quoted in Levine, *Half Slave and Half Free,* p. 162.

38. Quoted in Ward, *The Civil War,* p. 18.

39. Quoted in McPherson, *Battle Cry of Freedom,* p. 54.

40. Quoted in McPherson, *Battle Cry of Freedom,* p. 84.

41. Quoted in Levine, *Half Slave and Half Free,* p. 188.

42. Quoted in Levine, *Half Slave and Half Free,* p. 193.

43. Quoted in Ward, *The Civil War,* p. 24.

44. Quoted in Levine, *Half Slave and Half Free,* p. 211.

Chapter 3: Watershed Year: 1860

45. Quoted in Sandburg, *Abraham Lincoln,* p. 157.

46. Quoted in McPherson, *Battle Cry of Freedom,* p. 209.

47. Quoted in McPherson, *Battle Cry of Freedom,* p. 209.

48. Quoted in Ward, *The Civil War,* p. 6.

49. Quoted in Ward, *The Civil War,* p. 210.

50. Quoted in Levine, *Half Slave and Half Free,* p. 215.

51. Quoted in Sandburg, *Abraham Lincoln,* p. 164.

52. Quoted in Sandburg, *Abraham Lincoln,* p. 165.

53. Quoted in Sandburg, *Abraham Lincoln,* p. 165.

54. Quoted in Levine, *Half Slave and Half Free,* p. 217.

55. Quoted in Burlingame, *The Inner World of Abraham Lincoln,* p. 251.

56. Quoted in William C. Davis, *Breckinridge.* Baton Rouge: Louisiana State University Press, 1974, p. 227.

57. Quoted in Davis, *Breckinridge,* p. 233.

58. Quoted in McPherson, *Battle Cry of Freedom,* p. 231.

59. Quoted in McPherson, *Battle Cry of Freedom,* p. 231.

60. Quoted in McPherson, *Battle Cry of Freedom,* pp. 229, 230.

61. Quoted in McPherson, *Battle Cry of Freedom,* p. 231.
62. Quoted in Ward, *The Civil War,* p. 24.
63. Quoted in Levine, *Half Slave and Half Free,* p. 224.
64. Quoted in Sandburg, *Abraham Lincoln,* p. 183.
65. Quoted in McPherson, *Battle Cry of Freedom,* p. 243.
66. Quoted in Hanchett, *Out of the Wilderness,* p. 47.
67. Quoted in McPherson, *Battle Cry of Freedom,* p. 253.
68. Quoted in McPherson, *Battle Cry of Freedom,* p. 253.

Chapter 4: Caught Between Both Sides

69. Quoted in Levine, *Half Slave and Half Free,* p. 232.
70. Quoted in Sandburg, *Abraham Lincoln,* p. 188.
71. Quoted in Levine, *Half Slave and Half Free,* p. 234.
72. Quoted in Levine, *Half Slave and Half Free,* p. 228.
73. Quoted in McPherson, *Battle Cry of Freedom,* p. 255.
74. Quoted in William O. Douglas, *Mr. Lincoln and the Negroes.* New York: Atheneum, 1963, p. 12.
75. Quoted in Ward, *The Civil War,* p. 33.
76. Quoted in Douglas, *Mr. Lincoln and the Negroes,* p. 12.
77. Quoted in Sandburg, *Abraham Lincoln,* p. 214.
78. Quoted in Sandburg, *Abraham Lincoln,* p. 212.
79. Quoted in McPherson, *Battle Cry of Freedom,* p. 273.
80. Quoted in McPherson, *Battle Cry of Freedom,* p. 273.
81. Quoted in Sandburg, *Abraham Lincoln,* p. 232.
82. Quoted in McPherson, *Battle Cry of Freedom,* p. 311.
83. Quoted in Sandburg, *Abraham Lincoln,* p. 233.
84. Quoted in Levine, *Half Slave and Half Free,* p. 239.
85. Quoted in William Friedheim with Ronald Jackson, *Freedom's Unfinished Revolution.* New York: New Press, 1996, p. 62.
86. Quoted in McPherson, *Abraham Lincoln and the Second American Revolution,* p. 30.
87. Quoted in David Herbert Donald, *Lincoln.* New York: Simon & Schuster, 1995, p. 317.
88. Quoted in McPherson, *Battle Cry of Freedom,* p. 312.
89. Quoted in McPherson, *Battle Cry of Freedom,* p. 312.
90. Quoted in Sandburg, *Abraham Lincoln,* p. 263.
91. Quoted in Sandburg, *Abraham Lincoln,* p. 264.
92. Quoted in McPherson, *Battle Cry of Freedom,* p. 353.
93. Quoted in McPherson, *Battle Cry of Freedom,* p. 354.
94. Quoted in McPherson, *Battle Cry of Freedom,* p. 356.

95. Quoted in Sandburg, *Abraham Lincoln*, p. 272.

96. Quoted in Sandburg, *Abraham Lincoln*, p. 280.

97. Quoted in McPherson, *Battle Cry of Freedom*, p. 500.

98. Quoted in McPherson, *Battle Cry of Freedom*, p. 503.

Chapter 5: The Emancipation Proclamation

99. Quoted in Burlingame, *The Inner World of Abraham Lincoln*, p. 105.

100. Quoted in Burlingame, *The Inner World of Abraham Lincoln*, p. 105.

101. Quoted in Burlingame, *The Inner World of Abraham Lincoln*, p. 104.

102. Quoted in Sandburg, *Abraham Lincoln*, p. 290.

103. Quoted in Sandburg, *Abraham Lincoln*, p. 290.

104. Quoted in Sandburg, *Abraham Lincoln*, p. 312.

105. Quoted in McPherson, *Battle Cry of Freedom*, p. 506.

106. Quoted in McPherson, *Battle Cry of Freedom*, p. 504.

107. Quoted in Sandburg, *Abraham Lincoln*, p. 319.

108. Quoted in Sandburg, *Abraham Lincoln*, p. 314.

109. Quoted in Hanchett, *Out of the Wilderness*, p. 94.

110. Quoted in Sandburg, *Abraham Lincoln*, p. 314.

111. Quoted in McPherson, *Battle Cry of Freedom*, p. 508.

112. Quoted in McPherson, *Battle Cry of Freedom*, p. 509.

113. Quoted in Sandburg, *Abraham Lincoln*, p. 315.

114. Quoted in McPherson, *Battle Cry of Freedom*, p. 510.

115. Quoted in McPherson, *Battle Cry of Freedom*, p. 502.

116. Quoted in McPherson, *Battle Cry of Freedom*, p. 557.

117. Quoted in Sandburg, *Abraham Lincoln*, p. 320.

118. Quoted in McPherson, *Battle Cry of Freedom*, p. 558.

119. Quoted in Hanchett, *Out of the Wilderness*, p. 97.

120. Quoted in Hanchett, *Out of the Wilderness*, p. 97.

121. Quoted in Sandburg, *Abraham Lincoln*, p. 321.

122. Quoted in McPherson, *Battle Cry of Freedom*, p. 558.

123. Quoted in Sandburg, *Abraham Lincoln*, p. 344.

124. Quoted in Sandburg, *Abraham Lincoln*, p. 345.

125. Quoted in Sandburg, *Abraham Lincoln*, p. 347.

126. Quoted in Sandburg, *Abraham Lincoln*, p. 346.

127. Quoted in Sandburg, *Abraham Lincoln*, p. 346.

128. Quoted in Sandburg, *Abraham Lincoln*, p. 347.

129. Quoted in Douglas, *Mr. Lincoln and the Negroes*, p. 54.

Chapter 6: The End of a Long, Bloody Road

130. Quoted in Douglas, *Mr. Lincoln and the Negroes*, p. 56.
131. Quoted in Ward, *The Civil War*, p. 246.
132. Quoted in McPherson, *Battle Cry of Freedom*, p. 793.
133. Quoted in Sandburg, *Abraham Lincoln*, p. 380.
134. Quoted in McPherson, *Battle Cry of Freedom*, p. 565.
135. Quoted in McPherson, *Battle Cry of Freedom*, p. 686.
136. Quoted in Sandburg, *Abraham Lincoln*, p. 506.
137. Quoted in Ward, *The Civil War*, p. 335.
138. Quoted in Ward, *The Civil War*, p. 247.
139. Quoted in McPherson, *Battle Cry of Freedom*, p. 609.
140. Quoted in McPherson, *Battle Cry of Freedom*, p. 687.
141. Quoted in McPherson, *Battle Cry of Freedom*, p. 688.
142. Quoted in Sandburg, *Abraham Lincoln*, p. 450.
143. Quoted in Sandburg, *Abraham Lincoln*, p. 385.
144. Quoted in McPherson, *Abraham Lincoln and the Second American Revolution*, p. 122.
145. Quoted in McPherson, *Battle Cry of Freedom*, p. 762.
146. Quoted in McPherson, *Abraham Lincoln and the Second American Revolution*, p. 89.
147. Quoted in McPherson, *Abraham Lincoln and the Second American Revolution*, p. 89.
148. Quoted in McPherson, *Battle Cry of Freedom*, p. 775.
149. Quoted in Douglas, *Mr. Lincoln and the Negroes*, p. 62.
150. Quoted in Sandburg, *Abraham Lincoln*, p. 646.

Epilogue: Out of the Ashes

151. Quoted in Ward, *The Civil War*, p. 253.
152. Quoted in Ward, *The Civil War*, p. 347.
153. Quoted in McPherson, *Battle Cry of Freedom*, p. 846.

☆ Chronology of Events ☆

1619

August: The first African slaves are brought to America.

1775–1781

The Revolutionary War is fought; many blacks fight on the side of the colonies.

1780

Northern states begin abolishing slavery.

1787

Slavery compromises during the Constitutional Convention include a provision that a slave counts as only three-fifths of a person in terms of a state's population.

1793

Eli Whitney invents the cotton gin, transforming cotton from an occasional crop to one that ultimately fuels the South's economy.

1820

The Missouri Compromise allows Missouri to enter the Union as a slave state and Maine as a free state, and forbids slavery north of the 36 30' latitude.

1829

David Walker, a free black living in Boston, publishes his *Appeal,* urging slave resistance to slavery.

1831

William Lloyd Garrison begins publishing the abolitionist newspaper the *Liberator.*

1832

South Carolina threatens to secede from the Union, ostensibly over unhappiness with the tariff, but in reality their grievance is over the growing antislavery feeling in the North; the state backs down when President Andrew Jackson threatens to use force against them.

1846–1848

The Mexican War. At its conclusion, the United States gains a substantial amount of territory in the Southwest.

1846

David Wilmot, a Pennsylvania congressman, introduces his Wilmot Proviso, which forbids slavery in any new territories obtained from Mexico.

1850

The Compromise of 1850, which enables California to enter the Union as a free state but also produces a harsh new Fugitive Slave Law that makes it extremely easy for a master or his agent to hunt down escaped slaves.

1854

The Kansas-Nebraska Act is passed, which eliminates the Missouri Compromise's ban on slavery north of 36 30'.

1856

"Bleeding Kansas." Pro- and antislavery forces battle in Kansas over whether the state will enter the Union as free or slave.

1857

The U.S. Supreme Court issues its *Dred Scott* decision, which holds that slaves have no rights and that Congress does not have the right to forbid slavery in the territories.

1859

Antislavery fanatic John Brown leads a raid on the federal arsenal at Harpers Ferry, Virginia (now West Virginia), hoping to ignite a slave revolt and begin an antislavery guerrilla war.

1860

November: Republican Abraham Lincoln is elected the sixteenth president of the United States on an antislavery party platform.

December: In response to Lincoln's election, South Carolina secedes from the Union.

1861

January–April: Six more Southern states secede from the Union.

April: Confederate troops fire on Fort Sumter in Charleston Harbor, beginning the Civil War.

May: At Fortress Monroe in Virginia, Union general Benjamin Butler declares escaped slaves to be contraband of war.

August: The U.S. Congress passes the First Confiscation Act, which declares that owners will lose their rights to slaves used in the Confederate war effort.

1862

July: Congress passes the Second Confiscation Act, which declares that owners who participate in the war will lose rights to their slaves, even if the slaves are not used in the war effort; Lincoln confides to members of his cabinet that he has been considering issuing an emancipation proclamation.

September: Union forces win a critical victory at Antietam (Sharpsburg) in Maryland; in response to the victory, Lincoln issues a preliminary Emancipation Proclamation.

1863

January: The final Emancipation Proclamation is issued by President Lincoln; the historic document frees all slaves in Confederate-held territory and changes the focus of the war from restoring the Union to freeing the slaves.

July: Union victories at Gettysburg and Vicksburg turn the tide of the war in the North's favor; draft riots in New York City turn into race riots, in which blacks are targeted; the 54th Massachusetts, a black regiment, makes a gallant but futile attempt to take Fort Wagner in South Carolina—their bravery in the face of overwhelming odds helps change perceptions about blacks in the North.

1864

April: Confederate troops under General Nathan Bedford Forrest massacre black soldiers who have already surrendered at Fort Pillow, Tennessee.

September: After the darkest period of the war for the Union, spirits are raised when General Sherman takes Atlanta.

November: Abraham Lincoln is reelected president of the United States by an overwhelming majority over Democratic candidate George McClellan.

1865

January: The Thirteenth Amendment to the U.S. Constitution abolishing slavery is passed by both houses of Congress and sent to the states for ratification.

April: Richmond falls, and Lincoln enters the city and is besieged by freed slaves; the Civil War ends with the surrender of General Robert E. Lee's Army of Northern Virginia at Appomattox Court House; President Lincoln is shot by John Wilkes Booth at Ford's Theatre in Washington, D.C.

December: The Thirteenth Amendment is ratified and becomes part of the U.S. Constitution.

★ For Further Reading ★

Russell Freedman, *Lincoln: A Photobiography*. New York: Clarion Books, 1987.

Leonard W. Ingraham, *Slavery in the United States*. New York: Franklin Watts, 1968. A book that traces the evolution of slavery in the United States and also provides examples of how slaves lived.

Karen Judson, *Abraham Lincoln*. Springfield, NJ: Enslow, 1998.

Frank B. Latham, *Lincoln and the Emancipation Proclamation*. New York: Franklin Watts, 1969. A concise explanation of Lincoln's travels along the road that eventually led to the Emancipation Proclamation.

Robert Liston, *Slavery in America*. New York: McGraw-Hill, 1970. A book that traces the history of slavery in America, with emphasis on the slaves' suffering and the cruel system under which they worked.

James McCague, *The Road to Freedom*. Champaign, IL: Garrard, 1972. Another volume that depicts the course of slavery and what happened after it was abolished, covering the years 1815 through 1900.

John Anthony Scott, *Hard Trials on My Way*. New York: Knopf, 1974. A book that chronicles slavery and the struggle against it in the United States from 1800 up to the pivotal election of 1860, using diaries, songs, and other sources.

Dorothy Sterling, *Forever Free*. Garden City, NY: Doubleday, 1963. A book that traces both the history and growth of slavery in America, and the long, slow road that eventually led to the Emancipation Proclamation.

★ Works Consulted ★

Michael Burlingame, *The Inner World of Abraham Lincoln.* Urbana: University of Illinois Press, 1994. A fascinating volume that plumbs the depth of Lincoln's psyche to reveal the person behind the fame.

Bruce Catton, *The American Heritage Picture History of the Civil War.* New York: American Heritage/Bonanza Books, 1960. A lavishly illustrated chronicle of the War Between the States.

William C. Davis, *Breckinridge.* Baton Rouge: Louisiana State University Press, 1974. An excellent biography of one of the key political figures in American life during the Civil War era.

David Herbert Donald, *Lincoln.* New York: Simon & Schuster, 1995. A Pulitzer Prize–winning biography of the sixteenth president.

William O. Douglas, *Mr. Lincoln and the Negroes.* New York: Atheneum, 1963. Written by the late Supreme Court justice, this book not only explores the relationship between Lincoln and slavery, but also lists and explains landmark Supreme Court decisions in the areas of slavery and civil rights.

Shelby Foote, *The Civil War: A Narrative: Fort Sumter to Perryville.* New York: Random House, 1958. One of the finest and most in-depth volumes ever written on the Civil War.

John Hope Franklin and Alfred A. Moss Jr., *From Slavery to Freedom.* New York: McGraw-Hill, 1988. A comprehensive history of blacks in America.

William Friedheim with Ronald Jackson, *Freedom's Unfinished Revolution.* New York: New Press, 1996. An interesting attempt to present the Civil War and Reconstruction by presenting primary sources, such as letters and newspaper articles, and then letting the reader draw his or her own conclusion.

William Hanchett, *Out of the Wilderness: The Life of Abraham Lincoln.* Urbana: University of Illinois Press, 1994. An extremely easy-to-read, yet comprehensive, biography of Abraham Lincoln that covers all the significant events of his life.

Bruce Levine, *Half Slave and Half Free.* New York: Hill and Wang, 1992. A blend of social, cultural, and political history that explains the roots of the Civil War.

James M. McPherson, *Abraham Lincoln*

and the Second American Revolution. New York: Oxford University Press, 1990. A unique and interesting volume that examines Lincoln from the point of view of his speeches and public remarks, and uses them to explain his actions and decisions.

———, *Battle Cry of Freedom.* New York: Oxford University Press, 1988. This Pulitzer Prize–winning volume provides a wonderfully detailed picture of life before and during the Civil War.

Steven J. Rosenstone, Roy L. Behr, and Edward H. Lazarus, *Third Parties in America.* Princeton, NJ: Princeton University Press, 1984. This book contains information on all of the third parties in American history, plus an analysis of the conditions that give rise to third parties in American politics.

Carl Sandburg, *Abraham Lincoln: The Prairie Years and the War Years.* New York: Harcourt, Brace, 1954. Still one of the most detailed and comprehensive Lincoln biographies of all time, containing both the myths and the realities in a highly readable and enjoyable blend.

Geoffrey C. Ward, *The Civil War: An Illustrated History.* New York: Knopf, 1990. The companion work to the celebrated public television series.

✯ Index ✯

★ Picture Credits ★

Cover Photo: Corbis/Bettmann

Corbis, 33, 36, 38, 41, 47, 66, 89, 91, 94

Corbis-Bettmann, 5, 7, 8, 11, 21, 23, 26, 29, 32, 44, 59, 65 (top), 77, 79, 81, 84

Courtesy New-York Historical Society/Dover Publications, Incorporated, 16, 19, 23, 35, 43, 51

Digital Stock, 37, 50, 53, 55 (bottom), 63, 64, 65 (bottom), 74, 80, 83, 86 (bottom), 92, 93

Hulton-Deutsch Collection/Corbis, 54

Library of Congress, 9 (top), 14, 25, 69, 71, 86 (top)

Library of Congress, Brady-Handy Collection/Dictionary of American Portraits, Dover Publications, Incorporated, 76

Massachusetts Commandery Military Order of the Loyal Legion and the U.S. Army Military History Institute, 27

David Muench/Corbis, 9 (bottom)

National Archives, 55 (top)

North Wind Picture Archives, 73

Prints Old & Rare, 46

Retouched photograph by Mathew Brady. Courtesy of the U.S. Department of State/Dictionary of American Portraits, Dover Publications, Incorporated, 68

☆ About the Author ☆

Russell Roberts graduated from Rider University in Lawrenceville, New Jersey. A full-time freelance writer, he has published more than 175 articles and short stories and six nonfiction books: *Stolen: A History of Base Stealing, Down the Jersey Shore, Discover the Hidden New Jersey, All About Blue Crabs and How to Catch Them, Endangered Species,* and *Ancient Egyptian Rulers.*

He currently resides in Bordentown, New Jersey, with his family and a lazy, diabolical, but cute cat named Rusti.